B

MISS MYRTLE'S GARDEN

by Danny James King

Miss Myrtle's Garden premiered at the Bush Theatre, London, on 31 May 2025.

MISS MYRTLE'S GARDEN
by Danny James King

Cast

Rudy	Michael Ahomka-Lindsay
Melrose	Mensah Bediako
Myrtle	Diveen Henry
Eddie	Gary Lilburn
Jason	Elander Moore

Creative Team

Director	Taio Lawson
Set & Costume Designer	Khadija Raza
Lighting Designer	Joshua Gadsby
Sound Designer & Composer	Dan Balfour
Movement & Intimacy Director	Yarit Dor
Production Dramaturg	Olivia Poglio-Nwabali
Production Dramatherapist	Wabriya King
Costume Supervisor	Ellen Rey de Castro
Casting Director	Jatinder Chera
Dementia Consultant	Dr Nathasia M. Muwanigwa
Botanical Consultant	Coral Wylie
Production Manager	Daniel Steward
Associate Production Manager	Josh Collins
Company Stage Manager	Catriona McHugh
Assistant Stage Manager	Laura Whittle
Stage Management Placement	Annabel Smeaton
Set Builder	Centre Line Fabrications
Production Electrician	Kevin James
Production Carpenter	Jay Williamson

For the Bush Theatre

Lead Producer	Nikita Karia
Dramaturg	Titilola Dawudu
Associate Director	Katie Greenall
Marketing Campaign Lead	Laela Henley-Rowe
Technical Manager	Jamie Haigh
Head of Community	Holly Smith

This production is generously supported by Charles Holloway OBE.

CAST

Michael Ahomka-Lindsay | Rudy

Training: Royal Conservatoire of Scotland. (Recipient of the ALW Foundation Scholarship).

Theatre credits includes: Herbert in *More* (MTFestUK); Olunde in *Death and the King's Horseman* (Sheffield Crucible); Jonathan in *Reverberation*, David Heard in *Choir Boy* (Bristol Old Vic); Clifford Bradshaw in *Cabaret* (Kit Kat Club at the Playhouse Theatre); Jack Kelly in Disney's *Newsies: The Musical* (Troubadour Wembley Park Theatre); Emmett Forrest in *Legally Blonde* (Regent's Park Open Air Theatre); Benjamin 'Benny' Coffin III in *RENT* (Hope Mill Theatre); Paul Stephenson in *To the Streets* (China Plate & Birmingham Hippodrome); Maugrim in *The Lion, the Witch and the Wardrobe* (UK/Ireland tour).

Radio includes: Michael in *Scratch That: Highlife Romance* (Theatre Peckham).

Short films include: Craig in *Fart Car*; Chris in *The Cosmic Order*; Shahbaz in *Shielders*; Jerome in *Demons*.

Mensah Bediako | Melrose

London theatre credits include: *Master Harold and the Boys* (National Theatre); *One Man, Two Guvnors* (Theatre Royal Haymarket); *Clybourne Park* (Wyndham's Theatre); *Piaf* (Vaudeville Theatre); *The Harder They Come* (Barbican); *Tobias and the Angel* (Young Vic); *Floyd Collins, Strike!* (Southwark Playhouse); *Showboat* (Royal Albert Hall); *The View from Nowhere, On the Ropes* (Park Theatre).

Regional theatre credits include: *Much Ado About Nothing* (RSC); *Driving Miss Daisy* (Barn Theatre); *Fisherman's Friends* (Hall for Cornwall); *Fast Cuts and Snap Shots* (West Yorkshire Playhouse); *Once on This Island, Oedipus, Respect, The Wind in the Willows, The Bodyguard, Driving Miss Daisy, African Snow, The Mountaintop* (tours).

Television credits include: *Andor* (Disney+/LucasFilm); *Death in Paradise, Y Swn, EastEnders* (BBC); *Romantic Getaway* (Sky); *In the Long Run* (Sky One); *Chasing Shadows* (ITV).

Film credits include: *Flavia De Luce*; *Wonder Woman: 1984*; *Mr Mzuza*; *Popular Unrest*; *Frank in the Baseline*; *Wee King of Nowhere*; *The Real Kathy Hayden*.

Diveen Henry | Myrtle

Diveen Henry is currently shooting a supporting role in Sky's *The Inheritance* and recently performed in *Wedding Band: A Love/Hate Story in Black and White* at the Lyric Hammersmith, directed by Monique Touko.

Recent screen credits include: Mike Leigh's *Hard Truths*; *A Day of The Jackal* (Sky); *Ridley, Tell Me Everything* (ITV); *The Power* (Amazon) and *Temple*, alongside Mark Strong. Prior to this, she had a leading role in *Manhunt* (ITV).

Other notable credits include: *All Or Nothing, The Thick of It*, and *Prosperity* (directed by Lenny Abrahamson).

Gary Lilburn | Eddie

Theatre credits include: *The Weir* (Royal Court); *Desire Under the Elms* (Shared Experience); *The Quare Fellow* (Tricycle Theatre); *The Man Who Had All The Luck* (Donmar Warehouse); *Calendar Girls* (Chichester Festival Theatre/West End); *16 Possible Glimpses* (Abbey Theatre); *Dr Faustus* (Glasgow Citizens); *The Cripple of Inishmaan* (West End/Broadway); *The Taming of the Shrew* (Shakespeare's Globe); *Trouble in Mind* (National Theatre); *Six Characters in Search of a Good Night's Sleep* (Southwark Playhouse); and *Autumn* (Park Theatre).

Screen credits include: Joel Schumaker's *Veronica Guerin*, Stephen Frears's *Philomena*, and Lenny Abrahamson's *Garage*.

He will be seen in *Mr Bigstuff Series 2* (Sky) and *Babies* (BBC). He plays Des in Sharon Horgan's hit series *Catastrophe* (Channel 4). Other television credits include: *Bad Sisters* (Series 1 & 2); *Silent Witness, Mrs Brown's Boys, Paula, Pulling, Casualty* (BBC); *Belgravia* (ITV); *Single Handed* (RTÉ); and *Pete Versus Life* (Channel 4).

Elander Moore | Jason

Elander Moore will star in BBC & CBS's upcoming series *King & Conqueror* and recently starred in the hit Netflix series *Kaos*. Other screen credits include: *Interview with a Vampire* and *Death in Paradise*.

On stage, he played the role of Craig Donner in *The Normal Heart* at the National Theatre, directed by Dominic Cooke and had roles in *The Watsons* at the Harold Pinter Theatre and the *Barber Shop Chronicles* tour.

CREATIVE TEAM

Danny James King | Writer

Danny James King is a London-based writer who got his start in theatre before moving into films. His first play *Bounty* was runner-up at the Alfred Fagon Awards and was given a rehearsed reading at Kiln Theatre the following year.

Before becoming a full-time writer, Danny worked in a number of different roles, and spent a lot of time in the House of Commons where he assisted various MPs and was able to meet a number of high-profile figures, including Jeremy Corbyn, David Cameron and the Dalai Lama. He spent 2016 in New York where he worked at *Out Magazine* during one of the country's most contentious elections. There he gained experiences which informed his creative voice and changed the trajectory of his career path.

His time in New York inspired a stint of stand-up comedy, and after opening for comedians such as Nish Kumar, Catherine Eohart, Larry Dean and Stephen Bailey, he decided to concentrate on his career as a writer, rather than a performer.

Taio Lawson | Director

Taio Lawson is Bush Theatre's incoming Artistic Director and the Genesis Fellow / Associate Director at the Young Vic. He was previously Associate Director of Kiln Theatre and has held Resident Director roles at Sheffield Theatres, the Almeida, and on the West End run of *Hamilton*.

Selected director credits include: *an unfinished man* (The Yard Theatre); *NW Stories* (Kiln Theatre); *HOME Digital*, *Home – Installation* (Young Vic); *Macbeth* (Royal Conservatoire of Scotland); *hang* (Sheffield Crucible); *White Devil* (East 15 Acting School). In 2026, Taio will direct *Seagulls*, a sharp contemporary Black British retelling of Chekhov's *The Seagull*, for Kiln Theatre, which he has co-written with Dipo Baruwa-Etti.

Taio is also a trustee for PiPA (Parents and Carers in the Performing Arts), the organisation committed to amplifying the voices of everyone with caring responsibilities in the performing arts, to change mindsets and working practices alike.

Khadija Raza | Set & Costume Designer

Khadija Raza trained at Royal Central School of Speech and Drama. Khadija won the Linbury Prize in 2017 and was Best Designer at the Stage Debut Awards in 2018.

Credits include: *Girl in the Machine, untitled f*ck m*ss s**gon play, Sundown Kiki, Love Reign, The American Dream 2.0* (Young Vic); *Peanut Butter and Blueberries* (Kiln Theatre); *The Secret Garden, Every Leaf a Hallelujah, Antigone* (Regent's Park Open Air Theatre); *Dugsi Dayz, A History of Water in the Middle East* (Royal Court Theatre); *Sonders, Funeral Flowers* (Roundhouse); *...blackbird hour* (Vital Exposure); *Augmented* (Told By an Idiot/RET); *Mixtape* (RET); *The Flood* (Queen's Theatre); *Julius Caesar* (Shakespeare's Globe/UK tour); *10 Nights* (Graeae/Tamasha Theatre/Bush Theatre); *Bach & Sons* (Bridge Theatre); *Skin Hunger* (Dante or Die); *The Bee in Me, Great Ormond Street Hospital – Binaural Project* (Unicorn Theatre); *Cacophony* (Almeida Theatre/The Yard Theatre); *Philoxenia, Hijabi Monologues* (Bush Theatre).

Joshua Gadsby | Lighting Designer

Joshua Gadsby is a lighting designer and creative collaborator working across theatre, dance and live art. He regularly co-designs set, costume, and lighting with designer Naomi Kuyck-Cohen.

Lighting designs include: *New Beginning* (Queen's Theatre Hornchurch); *Mom, How Did You Meet The Beatles?* (Chichester Festival Theatre); *Who Killed My Father* (Tron Theatre/UK tour); *The Beauty Queen of Leenane* (Theatre by the Lake); *Alice in Wonderland* (Mercury, Colchester); *Gulliver's Travels* (lighting co-design, Unicorn); *Robin Hood: Legend of the Forgotten Forest* (Bristol Old Vic); *Cat on a Hot Tin Roof* (Leicester Curve/ETT tour); *in a word* (Young Vic); *A Kettle of Fish* (The Yard Theatre); *Tyler Sisters, Alligators* (Hampstead); *Still Ill* (New Diorama/Kandinksy); *As We Like It, Dragging Words, In Good Company* (The Place); *RISE: Macro vs. Micro* (Old Vic New Voices).

Co-designs include: *The Winston Machine* (New Diorama); *There is a Light That Never Goes Out: Scenes from the Luddite Rebellion* (Royal Exchange); *Trainers* (Gate Theatre); *Dinomania, Trap Street* (also Schaubühne, Berlin) both for Kandinsky at the New Diorama.

Dan Balfour | Sound Designer & Composer

Dan Balfour is an Olivier Award-nominated sound designer.

Credits include: *Dear England* (National Theatre/West End); *More Life* (Royal Court); *The Cherry Orchard* (Donmar Warehouse/St. Ann's Warehouse, New York); *Vanya* (West End/Lucille Lortel, New York); *A Christmas Carol* (Northern Stage); *Wuthering Heights* (Royal & Derngate); *The Dance of Death* (Theatre Royal Bath/UK tour); *Private Peaceful* (Nottingham Playhouse/UK tour); *Pavilion* (Theatr Clwyd); *hang* (Sheffield Crucible); *Idyll, One of Them Ones, Make Good: The Post Office Scandal* (Pentabus); *Effigies of Wickedness* (Gate Theatre); *Counting Sheep* (Belarus Free Theatre); *Voices of the Earth* (Complicité); *VINOVAT,-Ä, How to Break Out of a Detention Centre, Illegalised* (BÉZNĂ); *The Misfortune of the English, The Sugar Syndrome* (The Orange Tree); *Tempest* (Islington Pleasance); *The Hatchling* (Trigger Productions); *Two Character Play, Wilderness* (Hampstead Theatre); *HOME* (Young Vic); *Operation Mincemeat* (Splitlip); *The Double Act, Great Apes* (Arcola); *Dear Annie, I Hate You* (Riverside Studios).

Yarit Dor | Movement & Intimacy Director

Yarit Dor is co-director of Moving Body Arts company and is a movement director, certified intimacy director/coordinator and fight director.

Theatre credits include: *The Years* (West End/Almeida Theatre); *Fiddler on the Roof* (Regent's Park Open Air Theatre); *Why Am I So Single?* (Garrick Theatre); *Look Back in Anger, Roots, "Daddy": A Melodrama* (Almeida Theatre); *Othello, Henry V, Hamlet, As You Like It, Much Ado About Nothing* (Shakespeare's Globe); *A Strange Loop* (Barbican); *Hamilton* (Victoria Palace); *Hadestown* (West End); *Rockets and Blue Lights* (National Theatre); *Death of a Salesman* (West End/Young Vic); *The Band's Visit, Love and Other Acts of Violence* (Donmar Warehouse); *The Homecoming, The Second Woman, Changing Destiny* (Young Vic); *Black Superhero, This Is Not Who I Am* (Royal Court); *Old Bridge, Strange Fruit* (Bush Theatre); *A View from the Bridge* (Headlong).

Dance credits include: *Peaky Blinders, Rooms, Weather is Sweet, Goat* (Rambert Dance); *The Burnt City* (Punchdrunk).

Film/TV credits include: *Wicked, Supacell, Rivals, Atlanta, Rings of Power, Mood*.

Ellen Rey de Castro | Costume Supervisor

Ellen Rey de Castro is a British Peruvian costume supervisor and designer.

Credits include: *The Cardinal* (Southwark Playhouse); *The Sleeping Beauty* (Royal Opera House); *My Father's Fable* (Bush Theatre); *The Jungle Book* (Theatre by the Lake); *Sonder(s) by Centre 59* (Roundhouse) and *Scenes from a Repatriation* (Royal Court).

Jatinder Chera | Casting Director

For the Bush: *Lavender, Hyacinth, Violet, Yew*, *The Real Ones*, *A Playlist for the Revolution*, *Sleepova*, *The P Word*.

Other theatre includes: *Marriage Material* (Lyric Hammersmith); *Scenes from a Repatriation*, *G* (Royal Court); *The Comeuppance* (Almeida Theatre); *The Flea*, *Samuel Takes a Break*, *Multiple Casualty Incident* (The Yard Theatre); *Sweat* (Royal Exchange Theatre. Manchester).

Awards include: Olivier Award for Outstanding Achievement in an Affiliate Theatre (*Sleepova*); Olivier Award for Outstanding Achievement in an Affiliate Theatre (*The P Word*).

Olivia Poglio-Nwabali | Production Dramaturg

Olivia Poglio-Nwabali is a dramaturg, writer and arts producer based in London. She has worked extensively with the Young Vic – acting as the theatre's Associate Dramaturg between 2022 and 2024 – as well as with the Barbican Centre, the Southbank Centre and the Royal Shakespeare Company. Her work as a dramaturg is varied, collaborating on projects exploring diverse topics from palliative care to generative AI, and she is equally interested in devising experimental new work and reimagining canonical classics.

Olivia also writes and produces projects for the screen, and is co-director of a small film production company, Midnight Eye. She was a Barbican Young Film Programmer 2019/2020, and has acted as a production assistant on several commissions for Sky Arts. She is a volume editor for the book, *Decolonising the Theatre Space: A Conversation*, published by the Bloomsbury imprint Methuen Drama in 2024.

Daniel Steward | Production Manager

Daniel Steward is a graduate from the Royal Central School of Speech and Drama with a degree in Technical and Production Management.

He has worked as a freelance production manager across numerous London producing houses including Theatre Royal Stratford East (*Now, I See*); Hampstead Theatre (*Nineteen Gardens, The Habits*); and Queen's Theatre Hornchurch (*The Turn of the Screw, Bedroom Farce*) as well as working with Punchdrunk Enrichment (*Lost Lending Library*) and National Youth Music Theatre (*Into the Woods, Our House*). Daniel is also the current resident production manager for Punchdrunk Enrichment.

Catriona McHugh | Company Stage Manager

Catriona McHugh is a stage manager in theatre.

Recent theatre credits include: *Miss Myrtle's Garden* (Company Stage Manager, Bush Theatre); *Cymbeline* (Stage Manager, Sam Wanamaker Playhouse); *Girl in the Machine* (Stage Manager, Young Vic); *The Bounds* (Deputy Stage Manager, Royal Court); *For Black Boys Who Have Considered Suicide When The Hue Gets Too Heavy* (ASM Book Cover, Garrick Theatre); *HIR* (Company Stage Manager, Park Theatre); *Blue Mist* (Stage Manager, Royal Court); *Oklahoma!* (ASM Book Cover, Young Vic & Wyndham's Theatre); *Who Killed My Father* (Stage Manager, Young Vic) and many more.

Laura Whittle | Assistant Stage Manager

Laura Whittle is a freelance stage manager.

As Company Stage Manager: *Fly More Than You Fall* (Southwark Playhouse); *Wish You Weren't Here* (Sheffield Playhouse/Soho Theatre/tour).

As Venue Manager: *Pleasance Grand/Beyond* (Edinburgh Festival Fringe); *VAULT Festival* (The Vaults); *Underbelly La Clique* (Leicester Square); *Underbelly Lafayette* (Edinburgh Festival Fringe).

As Stage Manager: *Five Shorts* (Young Vic); *The Shivers* (New Diorama Theatre/schools tours); *The Light Princess* (The Albany Deptford/Arc Stockton/tour); *Captain Amazing* (Southwark Playhouse); *Pride London* (Leicester Square Stage); *Tapped* (Theatre503/tour); *Bangers* (Soho Theatre/tour); *Headcase* (Queen's Theatre Hornchurch/Trinity Theatre); *Snow* (tour); various productions with Moth Physical Theatre.

As Deputy Stage Manager: *Haringey Feast* (Alexandra Palace).

As Assistant Stage Manager: *Platinum Pageant* (The Queen's Platinum Jubilee); *Gin for Breakfast* (Tristan Bates Theatre).

Bush Theatre

We make theatre for London. Now.

For over 50 years the Bush Theatre has been a world-famous home for new plays and an internationally renowned champion of playwrights.

Combining ambitious artistic programming with meaningful community engagement work and industry leading talent development schemes, the Bush Theatre champions and supports unheard voices to develop the artists and audiences of the future.

Since opening in 1972 the Bush has produced more than 500 ground-breaking premieres of new plays, developing an enviable reputation for its acclaimed productions nationally and internationally.

They have nurtured the careers of writers including James Graham, Lucy Kirkwood, Temi Wilkey, Jonathan Harvey and Jack Thorne. Recent successes include Tyrell Williams' **Red Pitch**, Benedict Lombe's **Shifters**, and Arinzé Kene's **Misty**. The Bush has won over 100 awards including the Olivier Award for Outstanding Achievement in Affiliate Theatre for the past four years for Richard Gadd's **Baby Reindeer**, Igor Memic's **Old Bridge**, Waleed Akhtar's **The P Word** and Matilda Feyiṣayọ Ibini's **Sleepova**.

Located in the renovated old library on Uxbridge Road in the heart of Shepherd's Bush, the Bush Theatre continues to create a space where all communities can be part of its future and call the theatre home.

'The place to go for ground-breaking work as diverse as its audiences' Evening Standard

**bushtheatre.co.uk
@bushtheatre**

h&f
hammersmith & fulham

ARTS COUNCIL ENGLAND

Supported by
ARTS COUNCIL
ENGLAND

Executive Director	Mimi Findlay
Associate Director	Katie Greenall
Deputy Executive Director	Angela Wachner
Development Manager	Choi
Head of Development	Jocelyn Cox
People and Culture Administrator	Dorothy Ekema-Walla
Finance Assistant	Lauren Francis
Technical & Buildings Manager	Jamie Haigh
Producer	Emma Halstead
Assistant Venue Manager	Rae Harm
Head of Finance	Neil Harris
Marketing Officer	Laela Henley-Rowe
Lead Producer	Nikita Karia
Community Producing Assistant	Joanne Leung
Event Sales Manager	Simon Pilling
Senior Technician	John Pullig
Head of Development (Maternity Cover)	Marcus Pugh
Production Technician	Charlie Sadler
Venue Manager (Theatre)	Ade Seriki
Press Manager	Martin Shippen
Head of Community	Holly Smith
Senior Marketing Manager	Ed Theakston
Marketing Officer	Kelly Thurston
Marketing & Development Assistant	Amelia White
Assistant Venue Manager (Box Office)	Robin Wilks
Theatre Administrator	Pauline Walker
Café Bar Manager	Wayne Wilson

DUTY MANAGERS
Sara Dawood, Molly Elson, Thomas Ingram, Madeleine Simpson-Kent &
Anna-May Wood.

VENUE SUPERVISORS
Antony Baker, Addy Caulder-James, Emma Chatel, Zea Hilland,
Nzuzi Malemda, Roy Mas, Jacob Meier & Louis Nicholson.

VENUE ASSISTANTS
Javine Aduganfi, Doridan Bavangila, Manuel Ruiz, Will Byam-Shaw,
Pyerre Clarke, Daniel Fesoom, Matias Hailu, Bo Leandro, Maya Li Preti,
Ishani McGuire, Khy Matinez, Ed Mendoza, Carys Murray, Chana
Nardone, James Robertson, Ali Shah & Nefertari Williams.

BOARD OF TRUSTEES
Uzma Hasan (Chair), Mark Dakin, Kim Evans, Keerthi Kollimada,
Lynette Linton, Anthony Marraccino, Jim Marshall, Rajiv Nathwani,
Kwame Owusu, Stephen Pidcock & Catherine Score.

Bush Theatre, 7 Uxbridge Road, London W12 8LJ
Box Office: 020 8743 5050 | Administration: 020 8743 3584
Email: info@bushtheatre.co.uk | bushtheatre.co.uk

Alternative Theatre Company Ltd
The Bush Theatre is a Registered Charity
and a company limited by guarantee.
Registered in England no 1221968 Charity no. 270080

THANK YOU

Our supporters make our work possible. Together, we're evolving the canon and creating a bolder, more diverse, and representative future for British theatre. We're so grateful to you all.

MAJOR DONORS

Charles Holloway OBE
Jim & Michelle Gibson
Georgia Oetker
Cathy & Tim Score
Susie Simkins
Jack Thorne
Gianni & Michael Alen-Buckley

SHOOTING STARS

Jim & Michelle Gibson
Anthony Marraccino & Mariela Manso
Cathy & Tim Score
Susie Simkins

LONE STARS

Clyde Cooper
Adam Kenwright
Jim Marshall
Georgia Oetker

HANDFUL OF STARS

Charlie Bigham
Judy Bollinger
Richard & Sarah Clarke
Christopher delaMare
David des Jardins
Sue Fletcher
Thea Guest
Kate Hamer Ltd
Elizabeth Jack
Simon & Katherine Johnson
Joanna Kennedy
Garry & Lorna Lawrence
Phyllida Lloyd & Kate Pakenham
Vivienne Lukey
Sam & Jim Murgatroyd

Mark & Anne Paterson
Nick & Annie Reid
Bhagat Sharma
Dame Emma Thompson
Joe Tinston & Amelia Knott

RISING STARS

Elizabeth Beebe
Matthew Cushen
Anne-Hélène and Rafaël Biosse Duplan
Martin Blackburn
David Brooks
Catharine Browne
Anthony Chantry
Lauren Clancy
Caroline Clasen
Susan Cuff
Austin Erwin
Kim Evans
Mimi Findlay
Jack Gordon
Hugh & Sarah Grootenhuis
Sarah Harrison
Uzma Hasan
Lesley Hill & Russ Shaw
Davina & Malcolm Judelson
Mike Lewis
Lynette Linton
Tim & Deborah Maunder
Michael McCoy
Judy Mellor
Caro Millington
Rajiv Nathwani
Yoana Nenova
Stephen Pidcock
Miguel & Valeri Ramos Handal
James St. Ville KC

Jan Topham
Kit & Anthony van Tulleken

CORPORATE SPONSORS

Biznography
Casting Pictures Ltd.
Nick Hern Books
S&P Global
The Agency

TRUSTS & FOUNDATIONS

Backstage Trust
Buffini Chao Foundation
Christina Smith Foundation
Daisy Trust
Esmée Fairbairn Foundation
Garrick Charitable Trust
The Golsoncott Foundation
Hammersmith United Charities
The Headley Trust
Idlewild Trust
Jerwood Foundation
John Lyon's Charity
Martin Bowley Charitable Trust
Noël Coward Foundation
Royal Victoria Hall Foundation
The Thistle Trust

And all the donors who wish to remain anonymous.

If you are interested in finding out how to be involved, please visit **bushtheatre.co.uk/support-us** email **development@bushtheatre.co.uk** or call **020 8743 3584**.

MISS MYRTLE'S GARDEN

Danny James King

Characters

MYRTLE, *eighty-two, Black, first-generation Jamaican, moves
    slow but very alive behind the eyes*
RUDY, *thirty-one, Myrtle's grandson, Black, bookish type*
JASON, *thirty, Black, athletic, resting bitch face*
EDDIE, *seventy-five, white Irish, weathered, kind face*
MELROSE, *eighty-four, Myrtle's husband, Black, first-
    generation Jamaican*

Note on Text

A forward slash (/) indicates an interruption.

A dash at the end of a line (–) indicates a cutting-off.

*This text went to press before the end of rehearsals and so may
differ slightly from the play as performed.*

Prologue

The set shows a back garden in Peckham, clearly once cared for but now unkempt. There is a gate that leads out to the street on one side and the back of a house on the other. It's morning and MYRTLE *is sitting in her chair at the table.* MELROSE *can be seen tending the flower beds in the background.*

MYRTLE. I'm going out to come back.

> MYRTLE *doesn't move.* MELROSE *watches her. Beat.*

MELROSE. Well go on then, nuh!

MYRTLE (*calling*). Sarah?

> *No response.*

(*Calling.*) Sarah? Where you is? Sarah?

MELROSE. You still calling after her?

> MYRTLE *kisses her teeth and looks away. She eventually looks up at the sun, smiling briefly.*

MYRTLE. I'm going out the street.

MELROSE. You did say that, yes.

MYRTLE. Yes, well… You did see Sarah?

MELROSE. I'm sure she is nearby, Myrtle.

MYRTLE. All right…

> MYRTLE *gets up slowly and takes her purse from the chair.* MELROSE *watches expectantly as she walks towards the gate. Upon reaching the gate, she turns to him. They regard each other. She turns back to the gate and opens it. Suddenly, a thunderclap is heard.*

Ah wha' de –

ACT ONE

Scene One

Evening. MYRTLE *sits at the garden table with* JASON.
RUDY *paces around the garden.* MELROSE *continues tending the garden.*

RUDY. She can't be far.

MYRTLE. She can't?

RUDY. Well... I guess she can.

JASON. She'll turn up.

MYRTLE. Mm.

JASON. It's such a nice house, Miss Myrtle.

MYRTLE. It's all right.

RUDY. Guess how much her and Granddad paid for it? Six grand! Imagine!

MELROSE. Who tell the boy to go around talking about how much money we have?

JASON. It's amazing you could buy a house for that much.

MYRTLE. Amazing? Everything is amazing with this one. This house, the garden, the cuppa tea. Not everything can be amazing, Jason.

Beat.

RUDY. My point is, three months' worth of rent is how much they paid to own. Mad.

MYRTLE. Your rent that much?

RUDY. It's going up.

MELROSE. Lord, Jesus, what a life!

RUDY. Got to let our landlord know if we want to renew our contract by the end of the month. We live in a different world now, Nan. London's just unaffordable at this point. If we could save what we're paying on rent, we'd have a deposit in eighteen months –

MYRTLE. You two want to buy a house?

JASON. Yeah, / I think so.

RUDY. Loads of people buy with friends, it's not unusual.

JASON. Right.

MYRTLE. Look 'pon it. (*Motions around her.*) This garden is not what it was, at all.

MELROSE. I'm doing my best, woman!

MYRTLE. Yes, well… Your best and my best is not the same.

JASON *gives* RUDY *a look.*

RUDY. Are you okay, Nan? It's just, I heard Miss Pickett moved away.

MYRTLE. She never move away, them put her in a home. There's a young family in her house now. Them not so bad. Ugly children, but them not so bad.

RUDY. Do you still see Auntie Silvy?

MYRTLE. No.

RUDY. How come?

MYRTLE / MELROSE. She dead.

JASON. Oh my / God.

RUDY. Why didn't you tell me?

MYRTLE. I don't want to trouble you.

RUDY. But I… What about Uncle Sinclair?

MYRTLE / MELROSE. Dead.

RUDY. Humphrey? Bertram? Mr Payne?

MYRTLE / MELROSE. Dead, dead, dead.

RUDY. What about –

JASON. Rudy, maybe stop?

RUDY.... This house was always filled with life when I was growing up and now... I hope you don't get lonely...

MYRTLE. Lonely?

MELROSE *laughs*.

I wish I was lonely. Lonely would be nice. Lonely make me prosper!

RUDY All right, it's just a big house to manage on your own.

MYRTLE. It's not so bad. It's only the duppies that want to come trouble me and haunt up the place when them feel like.

MELROSE *kisses his teeth*. RUDY *grins at* JASON.

Why you look so?

RUDY. It's nothing, it's just... (*To* JASON.) Duppy means ghost. / Nan believes in... spirits.

JASON. I know.

MELROSE. And wha' wrong with that?

RUDY. There's nothing wrong with it, it's just... I'd like to think there are some things we can all agree on. Ghosts not being real is one of them.

MYRTLE. Yes, well... Maybe the duppies don't want to come to you, Rudy... (*Suddenly to* JASON.) You can garden?

JASON. Um... I've never had a garden.

MYRTLE. Wha' you mean? How you can never have a garden?

JASON. Just haven't. Always lived in flats.

MYRTLE. So you don't know if you can garden or not?

JASON. No...

MYRTLE. There's nothing to it... You get some soil... Some fertiliser... Plants... Flowers sometimes – you like flowers? And you just plant the ting...

JASON. Sounds pretty easy –

MYRTLE. Me never say that. It nuh easy. You must tek it serious, not everything can be easy easy all the time!

MYRTLE *kisses her teeth and looks away, hassled.*

RUDY. The other day at the school, we were talking about when our elders first came over and the students had a lot of questions. I was thinking it'd be good to talk about it at some point, if you want?

MYRTLE *ignores him. Beat.*

JASON. Maybe you should call the RSPCA? They might know what to do.

RUDY Good idea.

RUDY *takes his phone out and searches for the number.*

JASON. In the house... In case they say something we don't need to hear.

RUDY. Yeah... Okay.

RUDY *regards them momentarily, considering whether to leave them alone, before exiting.*

JASON. How long have you had her? Sarah?

MYRTLE *seems hassled by the question and then shrugs.*

I'm sure Rudy's right, cats don't tend to go too far from their homes.

MYRTLE. Yes, well... Maybe she dead too.

MELROSE. Maybe?

JASON. Oh God, really?

MYRTLE *shrugs.*

That's really sad. I'm sure that's not what's happened but you know, Rudy and I, we're not far. We'll be here.

MYRTLE. How you mean?

JASON. If you need a shoulder to cry on.

MYRTLE. Cry? You tink if I die, Sarah would cry for me? Wha' me must sit down and cry for? Me have Sarah here to keep the mice away and she can barely do that. Sarah would not be crying for me – Sarah would go about her business. Wotless cat!

JASON takes out his vape and inhales. MYRTLE stares at him. He awkwardly blows the smoke away from her and puts the vape away. MYRTLE looks away. Beat.

JASON. Rudy always talks about your curry goat. He loves it. I was gonna ask you if you wouldn't mind giving me the recipe? Rudy's a great cook but I'm still learning.

MYRTLE. It nuh easy.

JASON. No, of course not.

MYRTLE thinks. Beat.

MYRTLE. You can come round some time and me tek you through it.

JASON. That would be great.

RUDY re-enters the garden on the phone.

RUDY. They want to know how long Sarah's been gone?

MYRTLE. Not sure –

RUDY. Roughly?

MYRTLE. Since last night?

RUDY. Since last night?

MYRTLE. Yes.

RUDY (*into phone*). Sorry, I'll call you back. (*Hangs up.*) She's only been gone for a day, Nan! I thought she'd been gone weeks!

MYRTLE. Me never say that! She always here in the morning – this morning me can't find / her.

RUDY. You called me up and told me she was missing. Missing implies longer than twelve hours.

JASON. I'm sure she'll turn up, Miss / Myrtle.

RUDY. We've got to go. If she's not come home by tomorrow night, call me again.

MYRTLE. Yes, all right.

JASON *gets up to go with* RUDY *and they make their way to the back gate.*

Rudy?

RUDY. Yes, Nan?

MYRTLE. If you both need somewhere to stay, while you save that money, you can use the top floor. I never go up there anyhow.

RUDY. Really?

MYRTLE. Mm. There's three room. You can both stay here, I don't mind.

JASON. Wow, thank you, Miss Myrtle, that'd be amaz– That'd be great / and closer to work –

RUDY. Yeah, can I let you know?

MYRTLE *nods.* RUDY *goes and kisses her on the forehead. They leave. Pause.*

MYRTLE (*instinctively, without looking at him*). Why you look like that?

MELROSE. You coulda ask –

MYRTLE. And why I must ask? You never ask me when you throw away… Never mind.

MELROSE. Me don't mind Junior and him friend staying here but you shoulda ask for something.

MYRTLE. Why don't you ask him?

MELROSE *gives her a look.*

MELROSE. I'm just saying his mother would've charged him rent.

MYRTLE. Of course that woman would. Angela never care about no one but herself.

MELROSE. We could use the money right now, Myrtle.

MYRTLE *ignores him.* MELROSE *waves her off and goes back to his work.*

MYRTLE (*calling*). Sarah?

Scene Two

Night-time. MYRTLE *is in her dressing gown, standing in the doorway to the kitchen.*

MYRTLE (*calling*). Sarah? (*Beat.*) Sarah?

EDDIE (*offstage*).
And it's no, nay, never
No, nay never no more
Will I play the wild rover
No never no more

MYRTLE *looks confused as the drunken singing gets louder.*

I brought from me pocket ten sovereigns bright
And the landlady's eyes opened wide with delight
She said: 'I have whiskeys and wines of the best
And the words that you told me were only in jest'

EDDIE *appears in the alleyway of the back gate. He leans against the wall and begins to relieve himself.* MYRTLE *is incensed. She grabs the broom from the kitchen and goes to the gate.*

MYRTLE. Wha' ya tink this is?

EDDIE. Oh, I'm sorry – !

Before EDDIE *can explain himself to her she begins to hit him with the broom.*

MYRTLE. This look like toilet? My house look like toilet to you?

EDDIE. Myrtle! Miss Myrtle, it's me –

MYRTLE. Eddie? Ah you dat?

EDDIE. I-I'm very drunk and –

MYRTLE. Get out of my yard!

MYRTLE *hits him again and he leaves. She slams the gate and goes back to the kitchen door.*

Nasty, duttiness!

She re-enters the house.

Scene Three

RUDY *and* JASON *are sunbathing on the lawn.*

RUDY. I saw this great meme the other day that said...

RUDY *sees* JASON *is ignoring him and stops talking. Pause.*

All right, then.

JASON. All right, what?

RUDY. Let me have it. I know you're pissed with me, so let me have it.

JASON. I'm not pissed with you, I just – I don't want to be living a lie.

RUDY. Jase, if she found out, she might not want us in the house.

JASON. How do you know?

RUDY. I know her! She's my nan. My family... They're not exactly worldly and cosmopolitan, are they? You've seen her, you know what she's like.

JASON. She loves you. I don't think you're giving her enough credit.

RUDY. I get how things look from where you're standing, babe. But in the nicest way possible, you don't know what you're talking about.

Beat.

JASON. Mm.

RUDY. No, not 'mm'. You think I want to keep us a secret? When literally everyone in our lives knows about us?

JASON. It's just, if you're not out of the closet...

RUDY. Don't do that, Jase. I'm very out and proud in the rest of my life. What? Because I don't dress like Sam Smith you think I'm filled with self-hate?

JASON. First of all, no one should dress like Sam Smith. Second of all –

RUDY. It's 'secondly'. It's 'first of all' followed by 'secondly'. 'Second of all' isn't a thing.

JASON stares at him. RUDY raises his hands in surrender. JASON turns away.

JASON. *Secondly*, you are still holding yourself back if you're not being honest with your family. When I came out the closet –

RUDY. Jason, please! That closet had no doors.

JASON. – It was liberating! I had subconsciously been holding myself back in ways I never even considered. And yes the closet did have doors. My mum was very surprised.

RUDY. She was not.

JASON. Yes she was!

RUDY. Jason, she knew. She always knew. No matter how shocked she was, there's no way she was surprised. Shocked and surprised are not the same thing.

JASON. Why did I go for an English teacher?

RUDY *grins at him*.

RUDY. We just need to keep it up while you're in between jobs, that's all. It's called being discreet.

JASON. Now where have I seen 'discreet' before?

RUDY *chuckles*.

Funny how being discreet and being hidden feel like the same thing.

RUDY. And yet, they're not. I promise. Besides, saying yes to living here was your idea, remember?

JASON. Just because I say yes to something doesn't mean I forfeit the right to complain about it. And I thought we were gonna be in the big room. Why are we hitch up in the little room?

RUDY. It's not so little – listen. It won't be forever.

JASON *looks at him*.

Okay?

JASON. Okay.

They kiss. Pause.

RUDY. Also... I couldn't tell her you're Nigerian, so I just said you were from Trinidad instead.

JASON. So I'm not allowed to be queer and now I can't be African either? It's too much lying, man, pick one!

RUDY. The Nigerian thing would go down worse than the gay thing / trust me.

JASON. So while you're out here finding out about your history, I gotta wipe out mine? I'm buying those Prada trainers.

RUDY. No, you're not.

JASON. Who asked your permission, abeg?

RUDY. Trinidadians don't say 'abeg'.

JASON. I don't have my heritage or my identity, Rudy, so I will be buying those Pradas and you will find a way to live with it.

MYRTLE *enters from the kitchen, followed by* MELROSE, *who stands at the door.*

MYRTLE. And what is you two arguing about now?

RUDY. We're just joking around, Nan.

MYRTLE. Mm. Jason? You been to look a job yet?

JASON. I'm freelance, Miss Myrtle. I don't work every day, but I'll be out on Tuesday and / Wednesday this week.

MYRTLE. But why him never want to get a job?

MELROSE. The boy lazy, you nuh?

MYRTLE. All day, him just want to sit out here and yam out me fridge-freezer.

JASON *is about to respond but* RUDY *motions to ignore her.*

Just ah sit in the sunshine, like suh. You don't want to find a woman? You're not gonna find a woman out here –

JASON. God forbid.

MYRTLE. – Woman don't want a man who don't work. Woman want a man with some get up and go. But Jason! It seem like every time you get up, you sit down.

RUDY *laughs and* JASON *eyeballs him.*

JASON. Well, that's enough sunbathing for me. We need to get ready.

MYRTLE. Ready for what?

RUDY. You really want to go?

MYRTLE. Go where?

JASON. Yeah. I want an overpriced cocktail.

MYRTLE. You have cocktail money?

RUDY. Our friend has a bar opening around the corner –

MYRTLE. Where the fish shop used to be?

MELROSE. Them did a nice piece ah haddock.

JASON. I'm gonna jump in the shower and fling on a nice shoe.

MYRTLE. Him have a nice shoe?

   MELROSE *laughs*. EDDIE *appears at the gate with some
   flowers in his hand.*

EDDIE. Hello, Miss Myrtle.

   MYRTLE *jumps as she notices him.*

MYRTLE. Eddie? You know me can't tek the stench of drink so
   early in the day!

RUDY. Eddie? From up the road?

EDDIE. Ha! Toad of Toad Hall!

RUDY. Oh, wow.

JASON. What's that?

RUDY. It's what Dad used to call me. You remembered that,
   Eddie?

EDDIE. Of course! God, you're the spitting image of Rudolph.

   Awkward beat.

RUDY. That's funny, people usually say I favour my mum.

EDDIE. Oh really? I wouldn't have said –

MYRTLE. Wha' you want, Eddie?

EDDIE. I just wanted to drop these off, to say sorry, like. If you'll accept them?

MYRTLE *is silent.*

I'll just leave them here.

MYRTLE. What type ah flowers them is?

EDDIE. Daffodils. The ones you've always liked.

MELROSE. Is that right?

MYRTLE. Go tek the flowers!

JASON *stares at* RUDY. *He looks back. Eventually,* RUDY *gets up and takes the flowers.*

EDDIE. The other night I was drunk and... It won't happen again.

MYRTLE *nods.* EDDIE *turns to leave.*

MYRTLE. You can still garden, Eddie?

EDDIE. Garden?

MELROSE. Why you asking him? *I* can still garden, woman!

MYRTLE *looks at* MELROSE *and kisses her teeth.*

MYRTLE. There's some hydrangeas that want planting.

MELROSE. One hydrangea.

EDDIE. Well, you'd only need the one hydrangea, they're pretty big.

MYRTLE. You can plant them tomorrow. Come round at nine and don't be late.

EDDIE Oh... Okay. I um, I was supposed to be –

MYRTLE. Nine! And don't drink either. The smell ah bun' up me nose! Lord, Jesus, Eddie, how you let it come to this? Wandering around like a dog without a home. (*To* RUDY *and* JASON.) Him did used to tek care of himself, yuh nuh? Wha' happen to you, Eddie?

Scene Four

MYRTLE *is sitting in her usual chair while* EDDIE *and* MELROSE *tend different parts of the garden.* JASON *sits opposite her, taking notes on a pad.*

MYRTLE. Onions... Garlic... Thyme... Scallions.

JASON. What's a scallion?

MYRTLE. Scallion!

EDDIE. Spring onions, son.

MYRTLE. You did wash the meat?

JASON. Yes with cold water. And I put the salt and pepper on it already. Just giving it time to marinate.

MYRTLE. Salt and pepper hafi marinate?

MELROSE. What about all-purpose?

MYRTLE. You did remember the all-purpose seasoning?

JASON. Was I meant to put on all-purpose –

MYRTLE. But of course you must use the all-purpose seasoning.

MELROSE *kisses his teeth.*

You can do it later. The shop across the road have everything you need.

JASON. Okay. I'll be back in a minute.

JASON *goes to leave.*

MYRTLE. And you must hurry. You don't want the salt and pepper to marinate for too long.

MYRTLE *looks at* EDDIE *and silently laughs as* JASON *exits.* EDDIE *laughs too.*

EDDIE. That was wicked of you, Myrtle.

MYRTLE (*stops laughing*). Wha' you say?

EDDIE. I just meant it's funny –

MYRTLE. Mm, yes well… It's Miss Myrtle, Eddie, me and you is not family.

Beat.

EDDIE. You know you really remind me of someone I knew back home, she was always…

EDDIE *notices* MYRTLE's *ignoring him and stops talking, continuing to work. Pause.*

(*Singing softly.*)
I've been a wild rover for many's the year
And I've spent all me money on whiskey and beer
But now I'm returning with gold in great store
And I never will play the wild rover no more

Beat.

And it's no, nay, never
No, nay never no more –

MYRTLE. Eddie, quiet nuh! Me can't tek the noise!

EDDIE. Oh I'm sorry, m'dear, is the singing bothering you?

MYRTLE. It's a racket! You can't work in quiet?

EDDIE *works in silence. Pause.*

When you did become a menace to society, Eddie?

EDDIE. Well, I… I always enjoyed a few in the evening… Sometimes with Melrose, you know that.

MYRTLE. Yes well. You too old for that now, anyhow.

EDDIE. You're not wrong, Miss Myrtle. I'm much older than you are.

MYRTLE. Wha' you mean?

EDDIE. You don't look old enough to collect your pension.

Despite her best efforts, the compliment lands and she visibly softens.

MELROSE *turns and observes* EDDIE.

MYRTLE. Yes well… We have good genes in my family, fi true.

EDDIE. Absolutely.

MELROSE *reacts*. *Beat*.

MYRTLE. It's not so bad.

EDDIE. What's not?

MYRTLE. That song you was singing. It did have a nice melody to it.

EDDIE. D'you want me to sing it again?

MYRTLE. Me never say that.

MYRTLE *turns away*. EDDIE *continues to work in silence*. *Pause*.

When was the last time you went home?

EDDIE. To Cork? Twenty years or so…

MYRTLE. That's a long time.

EDDIE. I was planning to go back this summer. My sister keeps asking me and her lot are all grown up now. Got children of their own, like. Thought it would be nice to be part of their lives but…

MYRTLE. So why you never go?

EDDIE *shrugs*. JASON *re-enters through the gate with a carrier bag*.

JASON. I got onions, spring onions, garlic and thyme. I also picked you up some more all-purpose seasoning –

MYRTLE. You did get potato?

JASON. You didn't mention potatoes.

MYRTLE. But Jason, you never have curry goat? Of course potato is in curry goat! You never buy potato?

JASON *bites his lip*. *Beat*.

Jason?

JASON (*fed up*). Yes?

MYRTLE. You did buy potato?

JASON. No, Miss Myrtle, I didn't –

MYRTLE. Well you must buy potato. And then when you peel them you must remember to let them soak in water and not just leave them on the side.

JASON *goes to leave*.

JASON. I know how to do potatoes, Miss Myrtle.

MYRTLE. Oh, him can make potato? Well that's something.

MYRTLE *raises her eyebrows at* EDDIE *as* JASON *exits*. *Beat*.

You can make potato, Eddie?

EDDIE. Mary used to make a great stew every Sunday and I'd be on potato duty.

MYRTLE. Mary?

EDDIE. My wife. She was a very special lady. Beautiful. Smart. Always had a response to everything. We were married thirty years before she passed.

MYRTLE. You never tell me you was a widower.

EDDIE. I didn't speak about it. Melrose knew.

MELROSE. Him did tell me.

MYRTLE. I'm sorry to hear she did pass. Is that when you pick up the drink?

EDDIE. I always drank.

MELROSE. Him did always drink.

MYRTLE. And she put up with that?

EDDIE. She didn't mind.

MYRTLE. Then me and her is not the same. I could never have a man stumbling all over the place, slurring his word and stinking like a brewery. No sir! Not me.

EDDIE. She was a good woman.

MYRTLE. She would have to be, yes!

EDDIE. I knew her me whole life. One time, when we were kids, I was getting picked on by some of the other lads in the area. Tommy – he was their leader – he came up to me with his cronies while Mary and I were playing and he pushed me down and called me a faggot. The next thing I knew she had thumped him in the eye. He went flying!

MYRTLE *laughs*. MELROSE *gets up and sits in the chair opposite her.*

She told them if they ever touched me again she'd finish them – tiny little thing she was – and you know what they did? They ran off. Tommy O'Malley. What a wimp.

MYRTLE. O'Malley? What your last name is again?

EDDIE / MELROSE. O'Neill.

MYRTLE. Why them have to put O in front of everything? O this, O that? What a strange people you is.

EDDIE. I'll mention it at the next meeting, Myrtle… / Miss Myrtle.

MELROSE. Miss Myrtle.

MYRTLE. Myrtle is fine.

MELROSE *stares at* MYRTLE *inquisitively.*

Ireland don't sound too different to how I grew up in Saint Elizabeth.

EDDIE. How so?

MYRTLE. Just the same kind of bullies here and there. Growing up on the farm, it was me who did look out for my brothers and sisters.

EDDIE. You grew up on a farm?

MYRTLE. Yes. It was a big farm too. My father grew sugar cane, bananas, sweet potatoes, yams, plantains and what

have you. And we kept goats and pigs and cows. There was
this one cow, wha' her name was?

MELROSE. Mavis.

MYRTLE. That's right, Mavis. No one else like Mavis, but me
did like her. She was... my friend.

EDDIE. That sounds lovely.

MYRTLE. Mm.

JASON *appears at the gate.*

JASON. Got the potatoes.

JASON *re-enters with another shopping bag and walks
towards the house.*

MYRTLE. You did remember the Scotch bonnet?

JASON *turns on his heel, walks back to the gate and exits
again, wordlessly.* MYRTLE *gives* EDDIE *a look.*

Anyhow, what was I saying again? Ah yes, Mavis. So there
was this one time when a storm was coming and –

MYRTLE *suddenly stops in her tracks as* MELROSE *slumps
in the garden chair. She jumps out of her chair, panicked,
and watches him as he takes shallow breaths.*

MELROSE. Myrtle... Call an ambulance, Myrtle –

MELROSE *gasps for air as* EDDIE *goes to* MYRTLE.

EDDIE. Myrtle? Are you all right?

MYRTLE. Call for what?

EDDIE. Myrtle?

MELROSE. Call an ambulance, Myrtle!

MELROSE *has now passed out.* MYRTLE *stares at his
lifeless body.*

Scene Five

RUDY *sits at the table, writing in his notepad.* EDDIE *enters.*

RUDY. Morning, Eddie.

EDDIE. Morning, lad. What yer drawing there?

RUDY. Oh, I'm not drawing…

> EDDIE *nods, waiting for more.* RUDY *notices.*

> I'm doing my lesson plan for the week.

EDDIE. Ah. Teacher are yer?

RUDY. That's right.

EDDIE. Spend a lot of time planning lessons, do yer?

> RUDY *gives him a confused look.*

> No, it's just, you always seem to be at that table, scribbling away.

RUDY. Who doesn't like to be prepared?

EDDIE. Nothing wrong with it, lad. I knew a teacher once. Back in Ireland and he…

> EDDIE *trails off after realising* RUDY*'s not listening. Beat.*

> So how long have you and your fella been living with Myr– Miss Myrtle?

RUDY.…I'm sorry?

EDDIE. You and your boyfriend? Been here long?

> *Beat.*

RUDY. You think Jason's my boyfriend? No. We're friends. Flatmates. Our landlord put the rent up and we couldn't afford it any longer so Nan let us stay here.

EDDIE. That's good of her.

RUDY. Yeah.

EDDIE. She's a good woman. I wish I had someone to put me up.

RUDY *stops and looks at* EDDIE, *curiously. He nods and goes back to what he was doing.*

Sorry, son, I wasn't suggesting –

RUDY. I didn't think you were suggesting anything.

MYRTLE *appears in the doorway.*

MYRTLE. You did weed the garden yet, Eddie?

EDDIE. Yes, there's just a few more behind those bushes that are tricky to get to.

MYRTLE. Rudy, why you never help Eddie get the weeds from behind the bush? –

EDDIE. Oh, he doesn't need to –

RUDY. / I'm in the middle of something, Nan.

MYRTLE. You could help him for five minutes, it's not so long. Eddie's too old to be bending up himself behind the bushes. It's too much to ask?

RUDY (*getting up*). All right, I'll change my shoes –

MYRTLE. Eh, eh! What you have on your foot?

RUDY. These shoes?

MYRTLE. Where yuh find them shoes? Look at dem! Them look like clown shoes!

MYRTLE *laughs as* RUDY *looks irritated.*

RUDY. They were a birthday gift from Jason.

MYRTLE. I should've known he's responsible for this. Them look like the type ah shoe them wear in the sea – wha' them call them, Eddie?

EDDIE. Flippers?

MYRTLE. Flippers, yes! You look like you on your way to the seaside. Lord, Jesus!

MYRTLE *almost falls into* RUDY *laughing*.

RUDY. Okay, I'm going to get on with my lesson plan.

MYRTLE. You could pick me up some rock from the beach?

EDDIE. You do look like you could get work in the circus wearing those, son.

MYRTLE *stops laughing suddenly*.

MYRTLE. Wha' yuh say?

EDDIE. I said he looks like he could get work in the circus.

MYRTLE. Ah wha' me backside?! Wha' this coarse voice, dutty-lookin' jancro have to say about my grand pickney?

EDDIE. Oh Miss Myrtle, I didn't mean any–

MYRTLE. With him chatty, chatty self! Yuh face favour scarecrow but you wan' come cuss off my grandchild. No sir! Eddie, me can't support you with that! Me look like laughing stock to you? That's what him tek me for. Me and my family is laughing stock?

MYRTLE *kisses her teeth*.

Bright!

MYRTLE *turns and goes into the house. Beat*.

RUDY. So… Do you want to show me where the weeds are?

Scene Six

Night-time. MYRTLE *is sitting alone at the garden table opposite* MELROSE.

MYRTLE. You blame me, don't you?

MELROSE *is silent. Beat.*

I can see that… You can hide how you feel some of the time but not all of the time…

Pause.

I can only move so fast and… You couldn't move at all…

EDDIE *appears at the gate, just as* MYRTLE *begins again.*

But I am not sorry, Melrose, you is the one that left me, not the other way around. Me just ah sit here, minding my business and you have to come trouble me ah night-time! You go on like yuh haunted!

MYRTLE *suddenly notices* EDDIE.

Eddie?

EDDIE. Evening, Miss Myrtle.

MYRTLE. Evening is correct. Wha' you want?

EDDIE. I was just passing and thought I'd stop by.

MYRTLE. You can't garden at this time, Eddie.

EDDIE. Oh you're in one of your moods, I'll leave you to it.

MYRTLE. I am not in a mood.

EDDIE. You are. You never used to be this prickly. No, that's not true, you were always this prickly.

MYRTLE. Them did shut up all the liquor shop in Peckham and you drag yourself over here to raid my kitchen?

EDDIE. I've got me own drink, Myrtle.

He shows her his paper bag. She stares at him. Beat.

MYRTLE. You don't have shame, Eddie? Wha' you have in that bag?

EDDIE. Vodka.

MYRTLE screws up her face.

MYRTLE. That's why you smell so?

EDDIE. You can't smell vodka on people, there's been studies done.

MYRTLE. I can smell it. And it ah bun up me nose! You ever try Wray and Nephew?

EDDIE. Oh that's a bit strong for me –

MYRTLE. I will have a Wray and Nephew. You have one too. It's in the kitchen, in the cupboard by the fridge. Bring out two glasses.

EDDIE. You want me to go inside?

MYRTLE. I have a pain in my leg, so…

EDDIE goes in to prepare the drinks. MELROSE gets up and watches EDDIE.

EDDIE (*offstage*). I've told you to get that seen to, Myrtle.

EDDIE returns with the glasses and the bottle, places them on the table and begins pouring.

MYRTLE. Not too much.

He stops.

More than that.

He pours again.

Enough!

He pours himself one.

It's not cheap. You have your vodka for later.

EDDIE *puts the bottle down and sits in the chair opposite her. She registers he's sat down and looks to* MELROSE, *who looks disturbed before turning and going into the house.* MYRTLE *reacts.*

EDDIE. What is it now, Myrtle? You're a very difficult woman, you know that?

MYRTLE *ignores him.*

You don't think so?

MYRTLE. Think what?

EDDIE. That you're a difficult woman?

MYRTLE. Being difficult is better than being easy, Eddie. That's the problem, you men want women to be easy, easy and smile all the time. 'Oh, she's difficult'? So what? You want an easy woman, go find her.

EDDIE *smirks and then takes a sip of his drink. His face lights up and she grins.*

EDDIE. That is a lovely tipple.

MYRTLE. You see how your face light up? It taste better than vodka?

EDDIE. Much better. You were right.

MYRTLE. But of course.

MYRTLE *sips her drink and relaxes somewhat.*

So your wife… What was she like?

EDDIE. Mary? She was fiery. Like I told you before.

MYRTLE. You did tell me?

EDDIE. I told you she fought off those boys.

MYRTLE. Did she fight you too?

EDDIE. No. She was… gentle with me. We were gentle with each other. I've told you this.

MYRTLE. You never tell me.

EDDIE. Why were you talking to yourself? Before?

MYRTLE *is taken aback by the question*.

Sorry, if you don't want to say, it's just…

He trails off. Pause.

Plenty of people talk to themselves.

MYRTLE. I was not talking to myself, I was talking to Melrose. He was here.

EDDIE. Ah.

Beat.

MYRTLE. And you shouldn't go around eavesdropping all the while.

EDDIE. I'm curious about you, Myrtle.

MYRTLE. Yes well, you know what curiosity did to the cat? Oh, yes, the cat. You think curiosity kill her?

EDDIE. Maybe, if she asked you too many questions.

MYRTLE. That wotless cat.

They take another sip.

EDDIE. What does Melrose think? About your leg pain?

MYRTLE. Me don't want to trouble him with that.

Beat.

EDDIE. You will tell him I say hello, next time?

MYRTLE *looks away*.

So, what were you talking about?

MYRTLE *considers whether to share this*.

It's okay, Myrtle, I understand if you don't want to visit the past…

MYRTLE. I don't visit the past. The past visits me. And Melrose, well... Him nuh easy. Me tell him to come out of my yard, I don't want to hear it tonight!

Beat.

EDDIE. Does he come often?

MYRTLE. More now than when he was alive. At least when he was alive, you would find him at the betting shop or with some friends... He was sat there so, gasping for air and I couldn't help him, I'm not fast like that any more! I tried, I tried, to call them, and by the time them reach, him dead. But that is not my fault and it's coming like him want me to say sorry... But he was the one who didn't hold on. He was the one who decide to leave and I must grovel and beg him for forgiveness? No sir!

EDDIE. I'm sure that Melrose does forgive you. Even if it doesn't seem like it.

MYRTLE *looks away. Pause.*

I couldn't save Mary either. Cancer. I had to watch that parasite eat away at her until there was nothing left. Her soul was there but there was no life, you know? But she was still in there, somewhere.

MYRTLE. Mm.

EDDIE *looks at her. Beat.*

EDDIE. Of course, your son, I'm sorry, Myrtle.

MYRTLE. Go on.

EDDIE *thinks.*

EDDIE. The pain doesn't mature, I just visit it less as the years go by.

MYRTLE *meditates on his words. Eventually, she lifts her glass to him. He clinks his against hers and they drink. Momentarily,* MYRTLE *winces and rubs her leg.*

You all right?

MYRTLE. Mm. It'll pass.

MELROSE appears at the kitchen door and watches her. She looks at him.

EDDIE. You don't have to live with this pain, Myrtle. We can fix it, you know?

MYRTLE *considers this.*

Scene Seven

Night-time. RUDY *and* JASON *stagger towards the gate in night-club attire, clearly drunk and laughing.*

RUDY *(lowered).* All right, keep it down.

JASON. I wanna get into bed.

RUDY. Oh, I'm sure.

They go through the gate and JASON *grabs him and kisses him. They stare at each other.*

JASON. We're snogging… In Miss Myrtle's garden. The danger of it all.

RUDY. Are you getting off on this?

JASON continues kissing his neck and he pushes him back.

Okay, let's go inside.

RUDY *turns and goes towards the house.* JASON *pulls him back.*

JASON. Mm… Let's stay here.

RUDY. Jase…

JASON. What's the problem? We're in the shadows now, very 'discreet'… I'll be quiet…

RUDY. If she hears anything –

JASON. She'll what? Run into the garden and tell me I'm doing it wrong?

RUDY. Imagine. Actually, no, don't imagine.

RUDY *notices the kitchen door.*

Is the door open? Did you lock up earlier?

JASON. Yeah, I –

MYRTLE *enters the garden with a watering can.* RUDY *pulls away from* JASON.

RUDY. Nan! Did we wake you?

MYRTLE. No. The plants. Them have to water.

MYRTLE *goes to water the plants as* JASON *and* RUDY *watch her, perplexed.* RUDY *goes to her.*

RUDY. Nan, it's… the middle of the night…

MYRTLE. Hm?

RUDY. You're in your nightgown, give me the can.

RUDY *takes the watering can from her.*

MYRTLE. You want to do it?

RUDY. Eddie will be here in the morning. Let's just go to bed.

MYRTLE. Why?

MYRTLE *goes and sits at the table.* RUDY *looks at* JASON.

JASON. Tea? Would you like some tea, Miss Myrtle?

MYRTLE *shrugs and looks away.* JASON *enters the house as* RUDY *sits with her.*

RUDY. How are you feeling?

MYRTLE. Hm?

RUDY. Are you okay?

MYRTLE. I'm not so bad.

RUDY. 'Not so bad' still implies bad, are you sure –

MYRTLE. Why you have to do that? Pouncing on every word like a cat on a spider.

RUDY. I just want to make sure you're okay.

MYRTLE. Why?

RUDY. Because you're my nan.

MYRTLE. Mm.

RUDY. Okay.

> RUDY *leans back in his chair.*

> Whenever you want to talk, I'm here.

MYRTLE. Rudy, you is only ever concerned about me when you want something? You come over here with your little friend to help me find wassername –

RUDY. Sarah.

MYRTLE. And before I can even think 'that's nice', you're asking to move in –

RUDY. I didn't ask to move in!

> MYRTLE *gives him a look.* MELROSE *appears, wandering in the garden.*

> Do you want us out?

MYRTLE. Me never say that. What I'm asking is what you want now? Why all the questions and hand-holding and frowning like something is troubling you? You want me dead?

RUDY. What?

MYRTLE. I will be dead soon. You don't have to worry about that.

> RUDY *draws back and turns away, frustration written across his face. Pause.*

RUDY. I don't… That's not… I'm worried because you're not moving like you used to –

MYRTLE. I'm old!

RUDY. It's more than that! You don't communicate, Nan. You
never have.

MYRTLE. Wha' you mean by that?

RUDY. It's nothing.

MYRTLE. Wha' you mean?

RUDY. I ask you about the past, your history and you just
ignore me –

MYRTLE (*mimicking him*). 'History'! 'The past'!

RUDY. Every time! And worse, I've asked you plenty of times
about my dad. And you never want to talk about him.

MYRTLE *looks away.*

You're doing it right now!

MYRTLE. Sometimes the past is painful, Rudy! Not everyone
wants to live there, going over the same ting. I'm not going
to spend my last days raking over old graves just so you can
chat my business when I'm gone.

RUDY. I miss him too, Nan. I just want to know where I came
from. Who I came from. That's all.

MYRTLE *stares at him and points to herself.*

MYRTLE. I'm right here! Getting old is really something – Lord,
Jesus! You have people staring in your face asking you about
wha' happen instead of asking what's happening now… 'My
dad' – he was my son! My Rudolph was a good man!

RUDY. So then why can't we talk about him?

MYRTLE *goes silent again.*

You owe it to me to at least have a conversation –

MYRTLE. Rudy. I don't owe you anything!

MYRTLE *holds his gaze momentarily before looking away,
resolute.* RUDY *processes.* JASON *enters the garden with
a tray, putting it on the table.*

JASON. Okay, three cups of tea. Green for you, Rudy –

MYRTLE. Who you is?

    JASON *stops in his tracks.*

JASON. Miss Myrtle? It's me, Jason.

MYRTLE. Me nuh know no Jason – come out!

RUDY. Nan… What's going on?

MYRTLE. Rudolph, get him out of my yard! COME OUT!

Scene Eight

Morning. RUDY *paces as* JASON *watches him from the garden chair.*

RUDY. Do you think maybe she's…

JASON. She's gone to the shops, Rudy.

    Beat.

RUDY. I'm not overreacting.

    Beat. JASON *goes to him.*

JASON. Look, you saw the bottle of Wray on the side last night. She was drunk.

    RUDY *doesn't respond, deep in thought. Pause.* JASON *looks at his phone.*

    I've been thinking about what to do for your birthday next month.

    JASON *shows him his phone screen.*

    I think it could be good for us –

RUDY. I don't wanna celebrate this year.

JASON. You have to celebrate, you only turn thirty-one once.

RUDY. Thirty-one's such a nothing age, man.

JASON. What are you talking / about?

RUDY. Not now, my nan's gone AWOL and –

JASON. Rudy...

RUDY. I'm serious, Jase! She went to post a letter the other day and it was a whole production. She spoke about sending it for four hours, repeatedly asked me what time the postman works, put on about five layers in the heat, then took an hour getting to the end of the road and back. And now she's gone out? I'm telling you there's something wrong here.

Beat.

JASON. Okay. So, what should we do?

RUDY. I dunno. Call the police?

EDDIE *enters from the house.*

Eddie? How'd you get in?

EDDIE. Myrtle let me in.

RUDY. She's inside?

EDDIE. Yeah. We just got back from the doctor's. She had a pain in her leg, so I took her.

RUDY *is taken aback.*

RUDY. You took her?

EDDIE. Yes.

RUDY. Why?

EDDIE. She asked me. Anyway, she's gone up to bed. The doctor said... she needs her rest.

RUDY *looks at him curiously.*

JASON. That was kind of you, Eddie... Rudy?

RUDY. What?

JASON. It was kind of him to take her.

RUDY *is silent*.

EDDIE. I was just here and she needed someone. It's nothing personal.

RUDY. And you're sure that's all it was, a pain in her leg? He didn't say anything else?

EDDIE. Listen, son, it's not my place to tell you what Myrtle's doctor said.

RUDY. But he did say something?

EDDIE. Why don't you ask her? She'll tell you what she wants to tell you if you just talk to her… Take more of an interest in your nan.

RUDY. What does that mean?

EDDIE. I didn't mean anything –

RUDY. Yes, you did.

JASON. Rudy…

EDDIE. You know you're not so different, you and her.

Beat.

RUDY. I'll finish the garden off myself. I should be taking more of an interest, after all.

JASON. You can't garden!

RUDY *glares at him*.

RUDY. How much do we owe you? For the work you've done?

EDDIE. I don't want yer money, Rudy –

RUDY. Let's call it a hundred quid?

EDDIE *gets his jacket*.

EDDIE. I'll be back in the morning.

RUDY. I'm sorry?

EDDIE. It's up to Myrtle whether I do her garden or not. You're not in charge of Toad Hall yet, son.

RUDY is outraged as EDDIE goes to leave.

You might want to keep your phone on yer.

EDDIE exits. JASON goes to look at RUDY's phone.

RUDY. Can you believe that?

JASON. You have two missed calls.

RUDY. Who does he actually think he is? He's an old drunk who –

JASON. Rudy.

JASON gives him his phone. RUDY reads the message and then looks to JASON.

Scene Nine

Daytime. RUDY is gardening. EDDIE approaches the gate. They regard each other. Beat.

RUDY. The doctor said you told her to contact me… Thank you. Nan's had it a while, apparently.

EDDIE. I'm sorry, son.

RUDY. I'm not really sure what to do. Or what I can do even.

EDDIE. It can't be easy on yer. Or your friend…

Beat. MELROSE enters the garden. RUDY reacts to something passing him.

RUDY. She had it before Granddad died. Then she was alone… For years. (*Beat.*) Eddie… Why weren't you at Granddad's nine night?

EDDIE. We'd... lost touch. I lost touch with a lot of the old gang around lockdown. The drink...

RUDY *nods*.

RUDY. It was a beautiful night. So many people turned up, I wish he could've seen it.

MELROSE *smiles*.

I was talking to my Auntie Silvy that night and she was telling me how Nan and Granddad used to run a pardner. Granddad was that guy that would always help out if he could so people trusted him. But Nan was the one who kept track of it all and paid people out from week to week.

Beat.

She can fight this. I know she can.

EDDIE. We should sit down at some point and I can go over the different flowers with you.

RUDY. What?

EDDIE. They don't all need the same things. These are bluebells. I've put other flowers around them because they tend to disappear after their blooming season is over in spring... But for some reason they're still here. This garden seems to operate on its own time...

EDDIE *trails off. Beat.*

Myrtle's a strong woman, Rudy. She just needs the right care, is all.

MYRTLE *appears in the doorway, her face lighting up as she sees* EDDIE.

MYRTLE. Rudy! Why you never tell me him reach!

EDDIE. Good afternoon, Myrtle.

MYRTLE. Good afternoon? You alone cannot decide what type of afternoon it is. Me don't hear from you for how long? What am I supposed to do with this garden, hm? (*Tuts.*) Renk.

RUDY. Nan, you just saw him yest–

EDDIE. No, no… She's right. I'm sorry, Myrtle, but I'm here now.

MYRTLE. Yes, well.

MELROSE. It's *Miss* Myrtle.

MYRTLE *sits at the garden table.* RUDY *is somewhat frustrated by* EDDIE*'s assertion.*

RUDY. I've got to um… I'm a bit behind on my lesson plans.

MYRTLE. How much time you spend on these lesson plans, anyhow?

RUDY. It's never-ending, Nan. (*To* EDDIE.) You gonna be okay?

MYRTLE. Of course him is. Wha' wrong wit' you?

RUDY *exits, into the house.*

EDDIE. I shouldn't have left the garden half done, Myrtle.

MYRTLE. You was drinking?

EDDIE. A bit. I'm trying to stop that… Trying not to drink so much.

MYRTLE. Well at least you find your way back. Unlike that cat – Sarah?!

Beat.

Wotless cat.

EDDIE. It won't happen again. I'm going to finish the garden.

MYRTLE. You have anything to eat?

EDDIE. I haven't.

MYRTLE. That young boy, you know, the one who's a bit… (*Makes gay expression.*) Him did make some jerk chicken and rice.

EDDIE. How was it?

MYRTLE. It's not so bad. Him all right, really. You want to try some?

EDDIE. I'd love that.

MYRTLE. Come sit down, I'll bring it to you.

MYRTLE goes into the kitchen. EDDIE sits at the table.

EDDIE. They have some dahlias down on the high street. Six bulbs for thirty pounds, which is a bit dear, but I reckon I can get him down to twenty-five, twenty at a push. They'd go nicely by the tree.

MYRTLE (*offstage*). I never really care for dahlias. You did find the daffodils yet?

EDDIE. I don't know why you like daffodils so much.

MYRTLE (*offstage*). You don't need to concern yourself with why I like daffodils. What you have against daffodils, anyhow?

EDDIE. Nothing against them, they're just not my first choice.

MYRTLE (*offstage*). Well it's a good thing it's not your garden.

EDDIE. I was also thinking about planting some basil, rosemary and other herbs right by the gate there.

MYRTLE reappears with a plate of food and brings it to EDDIE.

MYRTLE. Basil? You can't plant basil in my garden.

EDDIE. Oh you don't like it?

MYRTLE. I don't want it here. You hear?

EDDIE. All right.

MYRTLE places the plate in front of him.

Oh wow, what a treat!

MYRTLE. It's all right. Me tell you the boy mek it and he did the best he could… Him best and my best is not the same but… It's not so bad.

EDDIE *takes a bite as* MYRTLE *sits opposite him.*

EDDIE. Delicious!

MYRTLE. It's my recipe.

EDDIE. You taught him well.

MYRTLE *stares at* EDDIE *as he eats.* MELROSE *enters from the kitchen. Pause.*

How's your leg feeling?

MYRTLE. So-so.

EDDIE. At least you got it checked out.

MYRTLE. That was good of you. You is a kind man. You always have been.

EDDIE. You think so?

MYRTLE. Oh yes.

EDDIE. I do my best. If you can help here or there, you're making the world a better place. Mary used to say that.

MYRTLE. Who Mary?

EDDIE *is about to respond then smiles instead.*

EDDIE. It doesn't matter. The point is, you're feeling better today.

MYRTLE. You've always taken good care of me.

EDDIE. Have I?

MYRTLE. But of course. That's why I married you.

EDDIE *stares at her.*

EDDIE. Myrtle... You've lost me.

MYRTLE. Mm.

An uncomfortable silence falls over them as he continues to eat.

EDDIE. I've er… I've been talking to my sister. I wanted to let you know that I'm thinking of going to Cork soon. I'll finish the garden first of course, but once that's done, I think I'll be making the move.

MYRTLE *stares ahead at* MELROSE *who is now tending the garden again. Beat.*

Myrtle?

MYRTLE. Hm?

EDDIE. I was just saying –

MYRTLE. You eat that fast. There's more inside.

EDDIE. Ah thank you, but that's enough for me…

MYRTLE. I didn't give you too much of the chicken –

EDDIE. No, it was grand, I –

MYRTLE. I didn't know if you would like it.

EDDIE. I do like it. Thank you, Myrtle, I really loved it.

MYRTLE *smiles at him. Beat.*

MYRTLE. I love you too, Melrose.

EDDIE*'s face drops.*

End of Act One.

ACT TWO

Scene Ten

MELROSE *and* EDDIE *are sitting at the garden table laughing hysterically.* MYRTLE *is watering the flowers.*

MELROSE. Myrtle! That's what you was doing, weren't it?

MYRTLE. Mm.

MELROSE. Wha' yuh mean 'mm'. You can't laugh about it? Why you have to be so serious all the time, woman?

MYRTLE. Me don't find it so funny, Melrose.

MELROSE *rolls his eyes at* EDDIE.

EDDIE. It was very funny, Myrtle.

MYRTLE. *Miss* Myrtle.

MELROSE *gets up and starts hopping from foot to foot.*

MELROSE. This was her. Hopping and skipping and jumping like so.

MYRTLE *hits* MELROSE.

MYRTLE. Yuh tink having mice is funny, Melrose? Me is laughing stock to you? And now you want bring shame to my house by telling the neighbours. What kind of person you is?

MELROSE. Me kill the ting, wha' more you want?

MYRTLE. You kill one! Them never come as one, them come as a pack. How me sposed to live in this squalor?

MELROSE (*to* EDDIE). You could never tell this woman grew up in Manchester, Eddie.

EDDIE. Manchester up north?

MELROSE. No, Manchester, Jamaica.

MYRTLE. St Elizabeth not Manchester – why you always do that?

MELROSE. Countryside is all the same to me.

MYRTLE. And what does Saint Elizabeth have to do with anything?

MELROSE. How you mean – Myrtle! The yard you grew up in had roaches and pigs and every other animal under the sun.

MYRTLE. We never had mice.

EDDIE. You want to get a cat.

MYRTLE (*to* MELROSE). You did tell him to say that, don't it?

MELROSE. Me never say nothing.

MYRTLE. Mm… Well, it's not gonna happen. Me don't want no dutty stinkin' cat in my house.

MELROSE The woman grow up in Noah's Ark but can't bear the idea of a cat.

MELROSE *returns with two beers and puts them on the table, offering* EDDIE *one*.

MYRTLE. What about you, Eddie? You can't chase the mice away for us?

MELROSE. Leave the man, nuh! Me never know why you don't like animal.

MYRTLE We're Black!

MELROSE. Plenty Black people like animals.

MYRTLE. Why you never want to sleep outside, Melrose? You is in the yard enough as it is, you may as well move your ting dem outer door and you can live with your lickle friend dem.

MELROSE. Me always did love cat. Them is not easy yuh nuh. You have to tek time with them. If them nah like you, them push up them face and turn away like so – (*Does face and movement*.) I tell you the reason you don't like them, Myrtle. You and them is just the same. Temperamental!

MYRTLE *laughs and smacks him.*

But them is also spiritual beings, yuh nuh?

MYRTLE. Not today, rastafari.

MELROSE. Listen... Them is known as a spirit guide. Them tek the dead to the next world. Lovely lickle creatures, dem is.

MYRTLE. What about you, Eddie, you like cat?

EDDIE. I can take them or leave them, Miss Myrtle.

MYRTLE. Mm. You is a decent man, Eddie. Him just want a cat 'cause him want something to look after, you hear?

MELROSE. You can blame me? Since Rudolph...

This strikes a chord with MYRTLE.

It could bring us some happiness, is all.

Awkward beat.

EDDIE. What yer cooking, Myrtle? Smells grand.

MYRTLE. Just some ackee and saltfish.

MYRTLE *sits down.*

MELROSE. Bun Up did call, you nuh?

MYRTLE *pushes up her face.*

EDDIE. Who's Bunnup?

MELROSE. Bun Up work down East Street Market – him real name Frederick but everyone call him Bun Up because him was in a fire as a child – so half him face bun up 'cross 'ere suh.

EDDIE. That's horrible.

MYRTLE. Him bun up so we call him Bun Up, Eddie! What else we must call him?

EDDIE. Frederick springs to mind.

MYRTLE *kisses her teeth.*

MYRTLE. Wha' him call here for?

MELROSE. Him did ask if he can join us to lay flowers at Rudolph's grave next weekend. Me tell him to come.

MYRTLE. But wha' me do to deserve this? You know me can't tek the sight ah Bun Up so early in the morning. Lord, Jesus, what a life!

EDDIE. I think you're being very cruel about Bun Up – Frederick, Miss Myrtle.

MELROSE. Listen… Him is good friends with Angela –

MYRTLE. That woman…

MELROSE. And since we not seen Junior in a while, thought it could be good to talk and find out how them is.

MYRTLE. Of course she fass up herself with his best friend but she can't pick up the phone and call, so we can speak to our grandchild…

MYRTLE trails off, seeing MELROSE look away defiantly. She in turn looks away. Pause.

EDDIE. Ackee grows on trees, is that right?

They look at him, momentarily.

MELROSE. You did want something to eat?

EDDIE. Well, if it's going, I'd be happy to –

MYRTLE. But you do look marga, Eddie. You must tek some food from the pot, yes!

MELROSE. Him do look marga, fi true.

MYRTLE. Marga! Go on, Eddie.

EDDIE gets up and goes to the kitchen. RUDY appears at the gate and enters the garden.

RUDY. Nan?

MYRTLE. You tink Rudy all right?

MELROSE. I don't know. That's what me want to ask.

RUDY. Nan?

MELROSE. You can live in contention, Myrtle, but not me.

RUDY. Nan?

MELROSE. I want to see my grandchild.

MYRTLE *rubs her hands, uncomfortably. Beat.*

RUDY. Nan?

MYRTLE. Rudolph?

RUDY. Rudolph?

MYRTLE. Is that not what your name is?

Scene Eleven

RUDY *stands in front of* MYRTLE, *who sits in her chair as* EDDIE *waters the plants.*

RUDY. I think I saw Sarah a few roads over. She ran past me when I was coming out of the shop. She was fast, but I'm sure it was her. She's nearby!

MYRTLE. Oh.

RUDY. I'm gonna get Jason and we'll search for her.

MYRTLE. No, no, that's all right.

RUDY. What? Why not?

MYRTLE. Sarah is not welcome here any more.

RUDY. She's not – ?

MYRTLE. She too out order! This is not a hotel. Thinking she can just turn up whenever she feel like and I'll be here waiting with a saucer of milk – no sir! She too forthright!

Beat.

RUDY. Jase!

> JASON *enters the garden.*

I saw Sarah.

JASON. Oh for real?

RUDY. Yeah, outside the corner shop. We need to go find her, she can't be far.

JASON I'll get my jacket.

MYRTLE. No!

RUDY. Nan, I know you're upset by her leaving but –

MYRTLE. Me don't want her here, I don't want her in my house! She is not welcome here, Rudy!

> MYRTLE *breaks down in tears and* EDDIE *goes to her as* JASON *gives* RUDY *a concerned look.*

EDDIE. Are you all right, Myrtle?

> MYRTLE *shakes her head and looks away.*

RUDY. Okay… We won't go to look for her, then.

JASON. Do you need a lie-down?

EDDIE. I'll take you, come on.

MYRTLE. Thank you, Melrose.

> *Discomfort falls over them.*

RUDY. Eddie, Nan… His name is Eddie.

> EDDIE *and* MYRTLE *disappear into the house.*

JASON. First me, now Sarah. I don't think she's in our world any more, Rudy.

RUDY. Well… She is for the most part. We just have to keep her rooted in reality.

> RUDY *sits and rubs his forehead as* JASON *comforts him.*

You were in my dream last night.

JASON. Was I wearing Prada?

RUDY. No.

JASON. Then it wasn't me.

RUDY. You were wearing a suit. I was wearing a suit. We were getting married.

Beat.

JASON. Sounds like just that. A dream.

They stare at each other.

RUDY. ...Jase?

JASON shakes his head and looks away.

JASON. I don't wanna talk about dreams, man. How long I gotta be asleep before I can live?

RUDY You're not asleep.

JASON. We are in a coma, Rudy!

Pause.

Is the money we're saving worth not being ourselves?

RUDY. It won't be forever.

JASON. I'm not interested in forever. I'm interested in right now. And right now, she needs proper care and we need our own place.

RUDY. With what money, Jase?

JASON. I don't know, Rudy.

RUDY. Exactly. So we just have to –

JASON. Tell her. About us. If you want us to stay, then tell her.

RUDY. Right now?

JASON. Yeah.

Beat.

RUDY. Okay. (*Shouts.*) Nan?

JASON. Rudy, what are –

RUDY. Shall I stick the kettle on and we can all have a big sit-down? She's losing her mind, but sure, now's as good a time as any –

JASON. All right!

RUDY *goes to him.*

RUDY. Look, I am working on getting us out of here... Are you in on Wednesday?

JASON. Yeah, why?

RUDY. I have an estate agent from Foxtons coming to value the house.

JASON *looks at him questioningly.*

I haven't told Nan, because she wouldn't understand but –

JASON. I don't understand either.

RUDY. The estate agent is coming to value it so we know what we have. If she does need the best care, then it might come to selling this place and it would be good to know what we can get.

JASON. We?

RUDY. Nan and I.

JASON. Oh... Okay. Then why can't Myrtle show them around?

RUDY. I'm not telling her, Jase, she'd think I'm trying to sell off her house before she's dead.

JASON. Would she be wrong?

RUDY *is visibly hurt and shakes his head, looking away.*

Do you think it's okay to be deciding these things without including her? How much should be her choice and how much should be yours?

RUDY *thinks.*

RUDY. I wish I knew.

Scene Twelve

Evening. EDDIE *is sitting at the garden table, drinking.*

EDDIE (*singing*).
I've been a wild rover for many's the –

MYRTLE (*offstage*). Stop yuh noise!

EDDIE. Oh, er – (*Raised.*) sorry, Miss Myrtle!

JASON *enters the garden.*

I've just had the one… And a half. Do you want to join me?

JASON *smiles and shakes his head.*

JASON. Miss Myrtle in bed?

EDDIE. Aye, she went up a while ago.

JASON. Okay. Thanks for staying with her, Eddie.

EDDIE. Ah, it's no trouble, lad. Now you're back, I can be on my way.

EDDIE *continues to sit and drink. Awkward beat.*

What have you been up to then?

JASON. Working.

EDDIE. Ah? Designing clothes were yer?

JASON. Styling… I'm a stylist.

EDDIE. What's that then?

JASON. Basically just… someone who dresses people I guess.

EDDIE. They have a job for that now'days?

JASON. Oh yeah. I mainly do celebs.

EDDIE. Anyone I would've heard of?

JASON. Do you read *The Shade Borough*?

EDDIE. No.

JASON. Then, no. It's a lot of keeping up with trends and speaking to soulless people… I dunno, I feel like I'm doing it just to do it half the time.

EDDIE. I understand.

JASON. Do you?

EDDIE. I was a tailor back in Ireland.

JASON. Serious?

EDDIE. Yes. It wasn't a fancy job or nothing. I used to just do fittings for cheap suits. People would come in feeling glum and leave feeling like a new person. My wife used to say that's what I was here to do: make people feel good.

JASON. That's nice. Styling isn't even what I wanted to do. I really wanted to be a designer but… I wasn't really good enough, so…

EDDIE. I find that hard to believe. Why did you stop?

JASON *shrugs. Beat.*

JASON. I don't know that I'm in love with it any more. Any of it.

EDDIE. Being 'in love with it'. That's a funny thing to say. People spend so much time thinking about what they're doing instead of just doing it. That's why I like gardening.

JASON. Because you don't think about it?

EDDIE. Yes, that, but… Plants are the opposite of people. They don't spend their time looking at the other plants around them, worrying 'oh no, I'm not as green as that one' or 'I wish I was as tall as the one in front of me'. They just are. They exist and grow at their own pace. We can learn from them.

JASON *meditates on this before* EDDIE *catches his eye.*

Ah, you're all right, lad, I've probably had too much to drink. 'Ere, I'll tell yer what. When you and Rudy get married, I'll fit your suits for yer.

JASON *registers this.*

JASON. You know?

EDDIE. Of course.

JASON. Good. I don't want it to be a secret.

EDDIE. It's not a well-kept one, son. You clearly care about each other. Dearly.

JASON We do. But we're not ready for marriage.

EDDIE. Oh no?

JASON. God forbid.

EDDIE. But you love him?

JASON. Yes.

EDDIE. And he loves you.

JASON. Yeah.

EDDIE. So what's the problem?

JASON. The problem is only one of us loves Rudy.

> EDDIE *considers this. Beat.*

Living here might be starting to drive me insane.

EDDIE. I remember when his father was dying. He used to visit him in that big room upstairs. Now he's back here but it's his nan this time. Poor lad.

> EDDIE *shakes his head.* JASON *digests this.*

JASON. Did his dad die in that room?

> EDDIE *is surprised by the question.*

...Why wouldn't he tell me that?

> JASON *is visibly hurt.*

EDDIE. Some things are harder to say than others.

> *Pause.* MELROSE *enters the garden from the house and takes one of* EDDIE*'s cans off of the table, going to sit on the grass.* JASON *watches the space* MELROSE *sits in thoughtfully.*

JASON. Does it bother you? Myrtle mixing you up with her husband?

EDDIE. Ah, I dunno. It's a part of her illness, isn't it? She's only mixing us up because she cares for me.

EDDIE *takes a swig. Beat.*

JASON. I'm just asking because I don't know that we should be ignoring it, Eddie.

EDDIE. She knows who I am. Most of the time. We have our own understanding, you know?

Scene Thirteen

Morning. MYRTLE *enters the garden.* MELROSE *is sitting at the table.*

MYRTLE. Why you keep hanging around here, Melrose? You don't have no friends in the afterlife? The spirits dem nuh like you?

MELROSE. You know why I'm here, Myrtle.

MYRTLE. Yes, well… I don't know why you leave just to come back.

Beat. MELROSE *is silent.*

You don't feel any type ah way about leaving?

MELROSE. You think it was easy for me? But it was my time! What must I do if the Lord is calling me?

Uncomfortable silence. MYRTLE *sits at the table.*

MYRTLE. You know where Sarah is?

MELROSE *stares at her. Beat.*

She gone. Rudy try to find her but…

MELROSE. Him can't.

MYRTLE *nods*.

But him did say she nearby, Myrtle. So you nuh have to worry. Soon come. But you is all right. You have Junior and... him 'friend'.

MELROSE *catches her eye. They silently laugh for a moment*.

But then you have your friend too.

MYRTLE. My friend?

MELROSE. Him look comfortable to me. (*Imitating* EDDIE.) 'Myrtle, what do you think of these roses?' 'Myrtle, let's go for a day out.'

MYRTLE. Ah yes. Our romantic trip to the doctor's.

MYRTLE *gives him a look*.

MELROSE. I'm just saying, Myrtle... You look all right to me.

Beat.

MYRTLE. I am not all right. I have a pain in my leg. And the whole heap ah the bills you left me with? And them dishes still have to clean –

MELROSE. Quit your complaining, nuh? Wha' happen to the carefree woman? The fun-loving girl? Wha' happen to her?

MYRTLE *stares at him*.

MYRTLE. Yuh out ah order.

MELROSE. Me?

MYRTLE. It is your fault why I am not carefree, Melrose! And then to come back from the dead and ask 'wha' happen?' Like a murderer returning to the crime scene and acting shocked. You know damn well wha' happen.

MELROSE. I see. You're still angry with me.

MYRTLE. Sometimes, yes... And it's not fair on the boy.

MELROSE. You should let him in, Myrtle. Talk to him.

MYRTLE. And say wha'? Him gon' hate me when I'm gone anyhow. When him find out.

MELROSE. But that's not your fault.

MYRTLE. That won't stop him from blaming me. He loves you too much. He'll be angry with me, not you. I can't let him in, if I can't be honest with him.

MELROSE. You need to prepare him, Myrtle.

MYRTLE. Why? Nobody prepare me.

MELROSE *considers this.*

MELROSE. You want me to say I'm ashamed? All right. Me feel shame, yes. But what can I do? The grief made you hard but it made me weak and...

MELROSE *rubs his hands uncomfortably.*

MYRTLE. Getting hard was the only way I could hold on to my dignity. One of us had to keep things together, and *you* chose me...

Beat. MELROSE *waits.*

Rudy... Him is so much like him father.

MELROSE. He's thirty-one. Lived more life than him too.

MYRTLE.... Why does his spirit never visit? Our son forget me?

MELROSE *is silent. Pause. A moment passes.* MELROSE *gets to his feet and conjures a portable radio. He starts fiddling with it before landing on an old song.*

MELROSE. You remember this?

MYRTLE *strains to hear but draws a blank.* MELROSE *starts dancing and holds out his hand for her to join him.*

MYRTLE. You never hear me say my leg is paining me?

MELROSE. Come on, woman!

MYRTLE *smiles in spite of herself and takes his hand, joining him. They dance together.*

You still move good!

MYRTLE. Some things you don't lose.

MELROSE. That's right!

MELROSE *spins her around and, suddenly, her housecoat becomes a ballgown. She marvels at it.*

MYRTLE. How'd you do that?

MELROSE. Beautiful!

MELROSE *pulls her towards him and they dance a while longer.*

MYRTLE. Melrose?

MELROSE. Hm?

MYRTLE. Promise me… Promise me you'll never leave me again.

Beat. MELROSE *pulls her in closer and presses his head against hers.*

MELROSE. Let's just dance, my love. Just for now. Let's just dance.

They continue to dance to the music.

Scene Fourteen

RUDY *paces nervously in the garden. Eventually,* JASON
arrives home and enters, hurt.

RUDY. I didn't expect you to turn up at the school, Jase.

JASON. Obviously.

RUDY. It's a Catholic school, you know that.

JASON. And?

RUDY. And… It's not that simple.

JASON. How do you think it makes me feel? To turn up there and
them not only not know I'm your partner, but not even know
that you're queer? And then you pretend that we're friends and
I'm just stood there thinking what the fuck? Am I a dickhead?
You can't tell me that Tilly and that other one would have a
problem – they're middle-class white women, abeg!

RUDY. If Tilly and Carla know, then the parents know, then
students are asking questions, then their parents are writing
petitions saying they didn't send their kid to a Catholic
school to be taught by a fucking faggot – I'm not a stylist,
Jase, people are trusting me with their kids, it's not the same
for you.

JASON. These parents exist in your imagination and nowhere
else. First of all, they already know. They all already know,
Rudy, you might not be as flamboyant as me, but you'd have
to be slow to not realise you're a 'fucking faggot'. (*Beat.*)
Have you stopped to think why you keep putting yourself in
situations where you can't be yourself? First your workplace
and now your nan's house. You could literally get a job at
any school and you go for the one where your sexuality is
going to be an issue? Why?

RUDY. It's well paid and I enjoy it.

JASON. Don't believe you, try again.

RUDY. You keep saying this 'being yourself' thing? I am being
myself there. What do you imagine me being myself looks

like? Should I be half-naked marching through the streets
with a pride flag at all times? Being gay isn't my whole
character.

Beat.

My work life is a different world, Jase. When I'm with you,
that's the real me. My job requires a different version of me.
So I play along with it.

JASON. And what about Myrtle?

RUDY. She gets another version of me too.

JASON. No, I don't mean that. What about her world? Why do
you correct her every time she calls Eddie 'Melrose'? It costs
you nothing to play along with that but you –

RUDY. Of course it costs me something! Are you mad? It costs
a lot. If she doesn't remember her husband, then did he even
exist? She's the last link I have left to my granddad... To my
dad! It doesn't cost you anything but for me the price is high.
And I can't afford it, Jase, I can't...

JASON *takes out his vape and inhales. Long pause.*

JASON. Do you remember the day we met?

RUDY. Of course.

JASON. That walk through Brockwell Park. Do you remember
me telling you how trapped I felt in my previous... I don't
even wanna call it a relationship. How he'd pick me up after
work. How he wouldn't pick up my calls because he was
with his family but he could call me whenever he wanted.
How it felt like I was frozen in time?

RUDY. I remember.

JASON. Well this might not be the same. But it feels the
same... It just seems like I'm never enough.

RUDY. You're *more* than enough, Jase.

RUDY *smiles at him. He doesn't smile back. Beat.*

JASON. I don't know if I wanna be in this garden any more, Rudy.

Pause. RUDY *meditates on his words.*

RUDY. What I remember about meeting you… is that at some point I just thought you were so much braver than I was. You felt very at home in your body… You felt like home to me.

JASON.… So did you.

RUDY. And I remember staying up late, chatting to ycu on the phone. Telling each other our darkest secrets and laughing when we realised we had all the same ones.

RUDY *goes to him.*

What can I do? Do you want to move into the bigger room? / We can –

JASON. What? No, no, I don't want you to do that.

RUDY. Okay, then tell me what I can do?

Beat.

Jase, why do you think I took the higher-paying job or moved us to this house? I want you to be the superstar stylist, I want you to focus on that even when it's not paying, so we need more disposable income. This is all for you!

JASON. I've never asked you for money, Rudy.

RUDY *lets out a yelp of laughter and shakes his head in disbelief, turning away.* JASON *stares at him, affronted.*

You think I have?

RUDY. 'Rudy, Maya Jama's gonna be at this party at The Standard, let's go get a few twenty-one-pound gin and tonics while I try chat to her.' 'Rudy, what do you think of these Prada trainers? Of this Versace shirt? Of this designer cravat?' Who even buys a cravat, man?

JASON. I bought all those things myself, so I dunno what you're talking about.

RUDY. And while you buy those things, I pay for everything else. You see how that works?

JASON That's not all the time and – why are you so pressed?

RUDY. I'm not pressed but the idea you've never asked me for money is ridiculous – like, be serious, Jason.

JASON. I think that's a story you're telling yourself.

RUDY. Oh, I'm sure you do.

JASON. You hear yourself, right?

RUDY. Do you?

Scene Fifteen

Daytime. MYRTLE *is sitting at the table.* JASON *exits the house wearing sunglasses, carrying his bags, and is surprised to see her there.*

MYRTLE. Jason?

JASON.... I'm going to stay with a friend.

MYRTLE. You and Rudy did fall out?

JASON. We're not really *friends* any more.

MYRTLE. Rudy never said nothing. You tell him you was leaving?

JASON. He knows... Ish.

MYRTLE. Ish? What is ish?

JASON. He knows I'm leaving, I just didn't say I was going so soon, that's all.

MYRTLE You didn't want to wait until him finish work?

JASON. No.

Beat.

MYRTLE. All right. Why you have them on?

JASON. What?

MYRTLE. Them. (*Points with her lips.*)

JASON. It's sunny.

MYRTLE. It's not so sunny.

JASON. My eyes are a bit red... I've been crying.

MYRTLE. Crying for what?

JASON. I... Look, I reserve the right to cry, Myrtle! Not everything needs an explanation. Is it over the top to be wearing these Mary J. Blige sunglasses? Maybe. But I'm hurt. And I don't need you or Rudy policing my feelings all the time!

Beat. He sits opposite her, taking the glasses off.

I'm sorry.

MYRTLE. You don't need to be sorry. I can see why Rudy likes you so much. You want some tea?

JASON *bursts into tears.*

But what do this boy now?

JASON. No, it's just... That's really nice. I would love a cup of tea.

MYRTLE. Yes, well... You'll have to make it. It's in the kitchen.

JASON *stares at her. She stares back.*

You think you're the first one to have problems? No sir! Me and Melrose did argue all the time. One night, that man made me so angry, I took that big heavy iron you see in the drawer there so, and me drop it 'pon him foot. You should have seen him, jumping about like him ah dance 'pon hot coal while him want to call me every name under the sun. We did argue, yes. One thing we never did was just up and leave. Children your age, you want to leave over anything and everything, but we did stay. The night Melrose left me for good... I did never get to say goodbye. And you can't just leave without saying goodbye to Rudy. That's not fair on him. And it's not fair to you either.

JASON *meditates on this. Beat.*

JASON. How long have you known Rudy and I are a couple?

MYRTLE *looks away. Pause.*

I've just been feeling like... I haven't been able to be myself for such a long time and if I stay here any longer I'm going to lose who I am entirely and...

MYRTLE *begins to cry.* JASON *is taken aback.*

Oh my God – oh Myrtle, I'm sorry, of course what you're going through is worse...

He kneels in front of her as she tries to shake it off.

MYRTLE. I don't remember him...

JASON. Melrose?

MYRTLE. No. No, him me can't get rid of and thank God for that but... It's my son I don't remember. And in some ways that's worse because... Because he was part of me. Life took him from me and now this ting in my head wants to do it again and...

JASON. I'm sorry, Miss Myrtle...

JASON *comforts her. Pause.*

It's a lot to deal with. And Sarah going missing must have been the last straw...

MYRTLE. How you mean 'missing'?

JASON. Sarah. I just meant, since she went missing –

MYRTLE. Wha' yuh ah talk 'bout? Sarah never went missing. She dead.

Beat.

JASON. Dead? Sorry, when did she die?

MYRTLE. Long time. The neighbours did find her in them garden must be… Must be… Wha' you bring up the cat for?

JASON stares at her. Eventually he nods.

JASON. Oh Myrtle… I'm sorry…

MYRTLE. Jason! You need to stop saying sorry so much! It's not everything you have to sorry for!

MYRTLE kisses her teeth and wipes her tears away as if the entire moment was a fever dream. JASON sits back down. Pause.

Your cooking is coming along nicely, though.

JASON. You think?

MYRTLE. Yes, well… Cooking is an art not a science. You have a talent for it.

JASON. Thank you! Rudy always cooked before so I just never really bothered.

MYRTLE. You can cook curry goat? We can do that next, I can show you curry goat.

JASON. Uh… Yes, I mean, you already… Yeah, you can show me tonight. I'll go to the market and get the meat.

MYRTLE. We can do that, yes.

JASON. Um… What did Melrose do?

MYRTLE. How you mean?

JASON. Why did you chuck the iron at him?

MYRTLE. Not chuck, drop. On him foot. And him, well…

MYRTLE reaches into her housecoat, takes out a bunch of letters and hands them to JASON. He looks through them.

Melrose was a good man but… him did have a problem with gambling.

JASON Oh my God! This… This is a lot of money.

MYRTLE. A lot of debt, yes.

JASON. How is… How's this going to be paid?

MYRTLE. They'll take the house.

JASON *lets the information descend on him.*

JASON. You haven't told Rudy?

MYRTLE. No… I don't know how to tell him that.

JASON. You have to, Miss Myrtle. I can't keep this from him. This is going to break him.

MYRTLE *nods. Beat.*

MYRTLE. What a life. I will tell Rudy. But you mustn't tell him what we spoke about here. About the two of you. That's for him to tell me. On his own time.

JASON. Yeah. I get it.

MYRTLE. He loves you, though. I can see that.

JASON *smiles at her.*

JASON. How does that make you feel?

MYRTLE. It's not so bad. At least you is not an African. That would break my heart.

Beat.

JASON. God forbid.

Scene Sixteen

RUDY *is standing opposite* MYRTLE *as she sits at the table.*
JASON *and* EDDIE *are waiting to go into the house.*

RUDY. We discussed this already.

MYRTLE. Wha' you mean discuss? Discuss wha'?

RUDY. I said to you we're turning the living room into your
bedroom so you don't have to keep going up and down the
stairs. So the sofa's going to the tip.

MYRTLE (*to* EDDIE). You did know about this, Melrose?

Beat.

RUDY. Eddie, Nan. His name is Eddie.

EDDIE. I... Yes, Myrtle, I knew.

MYRTLE. But how you just to agree to dash our stuff out on
the street?

EDDIE. I didn't...

EDDIE *looks to* RUDY *for help.*

RUDY. Look, let's just move it – we can talk about this later.

EDDIE. If she doesn't want to move it, son, I don't think we
should.

Beat.

RUDY. Jase?

JASON. I dunno, Rudy...

MYRTLE *looks disgruntled as she gets up and disappears
into the house.*

RUDY. What's the problem? She agreed yesterday.

JASON. When was the last time she recognised you as yourself,
Eddie?

EDDIE. What? I mean... She does and she doesn't.

JASON. But how long has it been since she actually referred to you as Eddie?

EDDIE I haven't been paying attention. What does it matter?

JASON. Okay.

EDDIE. What does that mean?

JASON. It means okay. I won't ask you any more questions.

EDDIE. Look, maybe we should just leave everything as it is. It's not like she can't walk. All this change might not be so good for her.

RUDY. It's not about whether she can walk or not, the nurse said it would make things easier.

EDDIE. Nurses don't always know what's best.

RUDY. They know more than us.

EDDIE. Are you sure you're moving her because of what the nurse said?

RUDY. What else would it be?

EDDIE. Maybe you want the top of the house so you and your boyfriend aren't disturbed.

RUDY *groans internally and takes a moment to compose himself.*

RUDY. No. We've moved her downstairs because it's apparently good to have everything on one level – hold on – in any case, if I wanted to move her so that me and my boyfriend can have the upstairs, what's wrong with that? Why are you so fass? Mind your business. I'm the one caring for her, Eddie, not you.

EDDIE. As long as you are caring for her.

RUDY *flashes his eyes at* JASON. *He nods in response.*

JASON. Eddie, we're not even going to be here much longer. We're looking for a flat. Hence the reason we're setting the place up for the nurse.

EDDIE. Ah. So you're moving out?

RUDY. Maybe, yeah.

JASON. Not maybe, Rudy, we agreed.

RUDY. I just feel like… what is the actual point in us moving?

JASON. What do you mean?

EDDIE. He means your nan will be dead soon so you may as well take over the house now.

RUDY. Fucking hell!

JASON disappears into the house.

What's the matter, Eddie? Jealous? Were you hoping to get your feet under the table so you can get your withered old hands on the house instead?

EDDIE. Unlike you, Rudy, I'm not here because I have ulterior motives. I'm here because I…

RUDY You what? Love her? Shame she doesn't know you from Adam.

EDDIE. She does know me! We know each other! I'm sick of you dismissing me as if I'm a deluded old man, we…

JASON re-enters the garden, holding the letters.

RUDY. She's got dementia, Eddie! It's got nothing to do with delusion and everything to do with a clear medical condition.

JASON puts the letters in RUDY's hands.

What's this?

JASON is silent. RUDY opens the letters and begins reading. RUDY processes. Pause.

This doesn't make any sense. Granddad promised me this house.

JASON. I'm sorry, Rudy.

An uneasy silence falls over them. Pause.

RUDY (*to* EDDIE). Are you laughing?

EDDIE. What?

RUDY. You're laughing?

EDDIE. I wasn't –

JASON. He wasn't laughing, Rudy.

RUDY. There must be a way to fix this, it can't just be gone.
Not after all this.

JASON All what?

RUDY. All this work! We've been looking after her this whole
time only for it…

> RUDY *trails off and then catches* EDDIE*'s eye.*

Fuck off, that's not what I meant!

EDDIE. I didn't say anything, son.

RUDY. I am *not* your son.

> MYRTLE *appears at the kitchen doorway.*

MYRTLE. Melrose?

> EDDIE *groans.*

EDDIE. Myrtle?

MYRTLE. I found it!

EDDIE. Found what?

> MYRTLE *smiles as she goes to him and shows him what's in
> her hand.*

MYRTLE. Your wedding ring. I put it in my drawer for safe
keeping, me did forget.

EDDIE. Myrtle, I um…

RUDY. Why not put it on?

JASON. Rudy, stop right now!

RUDY. Go on, Melrose. Put it on.

EDDIE. I'm not going to –

RUDY. Nan asked you to. Go on, Granddad.

JASON. Rudy!

RUDY. Put on your wedding ring.

MYRTLE. Put it on, nuh!

> EDDIE *stares at her. Beat. He takes the ring.* JASON *looks away as* EDDIE *puts it on.*

> What's wrong, Melrose?

EDDIE. I'm not Melrose, Myrtle! I'm not him! STOP FUCKING CALLING ME THAT!

> *Suddenly,* EDDIE *breaks down and begins to cry.*

MYRTLE. What did I do?

JASON. You didn't do anything, Miss Myrtle, come with me, we're going inside.

MYRTLE But why him look so…

JASON. It's fine, come on, we'll have some tea.

> JASON *escorts* MYRTLE *into the house, shooting* RUDY *a look as he goes.* RUDY *nods and battles with himself briefly before sitting beside* EDDIE, *who is crying uncontrollably.*

RUDY. Eddie? Eddie, I'm sorry. That wasn't… I'm so sorry.

> EDDIE *wipes his eyes and looks at* RUDY.

EDDIE. She doesn't know me. She doesn't know me. She never did.

RUDY. That's not true. She definitely did.

EDDIE. She doesn't now.

> RUDY *goes to put his hand on his shoulder but doesn't. Beat.*

RUDY. Do you want me to fix you a drink?

EDDIE. No… No, I don't think I want that any more.

RUDY. Okay… God, Eddie, maybe you're right… Maybe I am a terrible person.

EDDIE. You're not a terrible person, son – sorry, force of habit. It's just a saying –

RUDY. I know… I know.

EDDIE continues to sob. RUDY sits with him for a while. Long pause.

She's just confused, Eddie. It's a confusing time for her. The truth is, we'll never know how lucid she's been these past few months. But her confusion led her to you. That has to mean something. Right?

JASON appears in the doorway.

JASON. Rudy, I need your help with her.

He disappears again. RUDY gets up and goes to the house, then stops and turns to EDDIE.

RUDY. It has to mean something, Eddie.

RUDY disappears into the house, leaving EDDIE alone, staring at the ring in his hand.

Scene Seventeen

Daytime. RUDY *is watering the plants, carefully and methodically. He goes from one end of the garden to the other.* JASON *exits the house with his bags and watches him for a while, unnoticed.* RUDY *eventually notices him and they regard each other silently for a moment.*

JASON. Not this Alan Titchmarsh. What happened to 'I'm not a gardener'?

RUDY. It's not like I'm about to compete in the Chelsea Flower Show, is it? Eddie talked me through all the different types. So I can take over... Did you meet Jackie?

JASON. Yes, Nurse Jackie. Imagine.

RUDY. She seems like a good fit...

JASON. Yeah. So, go on then. Tell me about the plants.

JASON *walks to the flower bed.*

RUDY. Well... They're split between annuals, biennials, perennials and shrubs. Shrubs are my favourite. They're evergreen.

JASON. Evergreen. Lit.

RUDY. It's kinda interesting. Nature. Some things are meant to be evergreen and others have a specific life cycle and then...

Beat.

JASON. Did you speak to the debt companies?

RUDY. Yeah.

JASON. And?

RUDY. Has to be paid. No two ways about it.

JASON. I'm sorry.

RUDY *shrugs.*

RUDY. Anyway, some need watering once a day, others once in a while – that one's every few weeks. I'm making a spreadsheet to keep track.

JASON. Oh you love a spreadsheet. So how come the cactus doesn't need watering every day?

RUDY. I dunno. They're pretty tough, cacti.

JASON. Is that what they're called?

RUDY. Collectively, yes.

JASON. I'm gonna miss learning new words from you.

RUDY. Cacti is pretty basic, hun.

JASON. I'm not, however, gonna miss you being a condescending prick.

RUDY. You definitely are.

JASON. Maybe. Just a little.

They kiss.

Sure you don't wanna come?

Pause.

RUDY. I'm meant to be here. I'd be holding you back wherever we are, Jase. There's something missing for me. You know that.

JASON. I know. Me too... Did I tell you my new place has a garden?

RUDY. No, you didn't!

JASON. Communal, but still. Maybe I'll start gardening too.

They press their foreheads together for a while. Eventually they break apart and JASON *goes to get his bags.*

If you need any help, you can / call me.

RUDY. I know.

JASON goes to the garden gate and hesitates to open it. He turns back to RUDY *to say something and thinks better of it before turning and exiting.* RUDY *stands and stares at the gate.* MYRTLE *enters the garden from the kitchen, unseen by* RUDY. *A rustling in the tree gets his attention. He looks up at it and seeing nothing, turns to the kitchen, startled upon seeing* MYRTLE.

Hi Nan.

MYRTLE. What you was looking at?

RUDY. I thought there was something there but... Never mind. Jason just left.

MYRTLE I know. Him did tell me he was going back to Trinidad.

RUDY *laughs*.

RUDY. That sounds about right.

MYRTLE *sits at the table.* RUDY *stares at her. Pause.*

We just broke up. Jason was my partner.

RUDY *goes to sit opposite her.*

I, um... I need to tell you... I'm gay, Nan. I'm a gay man...

MYRTLE *nods. Silence hangs between the two.*

Are you surprised?

MYRTLE. Surprise?

She stares at him for a moment.

You think I was born yesterday? I've always known that, Rudy. You is who you is, and who you is, is a good man. You don't have to trouble yourself worrying about that... Surprise? What surprise?

MYRTLE *kisses her teeth and laughs to herself.* RUDY *is taken aback as he processes her words. Long pause.*

RUDY. How long... How long have you known?

MYRTLE. Known what?

RUDY *stares at her, his heart sinking. Beat.*

RUDY. It's nothing.

MYRTLE. It doesn't look like nothing, you look upset –

RUDY. It doesn't matter.

MYRTLE. You sure it doesn't?

RUDY *considers this and then slowly, he smiles at her.*

RUDY. It doesn't. It actually doesn't matter.

He laughs in spite of himself. Beat. MYRTLE *stares at him.*

MYRTLE. You look so much like your father.

RUDY. Wow. Okay.

MYRTLE. What was he like?

RUDY *is taken aback.*

RUDY. Dad? Oh…

Beat.

He was… kind and um… No, that's just something people said about him after he died. Let me think… What was he like?

RUDY *thinks.*

Okay, so there was this one time when I was at school, before he got ill, and he came to pick me up at the gates, and I'd been crying. He asked me what was wrong so I told him I got picked last for football. Keiran – who was my best friend – left me till last. It was humiliating. So Dad asked me if I liked football? I said not really. He told me there was no point trying to be like the other boys, that I was special in my own right. Then he took me to Peckham Library. He knew I loved books. It had just opened. I'd never seen so many in one place. He told me to pick one out to take back to my mum's… *The Wind in the Willows.*

RUDY *looks at* MYRTLE.

Do you remember anything about him?

MYRTLE. Not a lot. Just feelings. I remember he was a big, big man. A giant. But he convinced himself he was an insect. And I didn't know how to fix that. There was always something missing for him.

RUDY *nods, thoughtfully.*

RUDY. What do you think that was?

MYRTLE *shrugs and looks away.* RUDY *sighs.*

It's nice though, Nan... hearing you talk about him. If you're having trouble remembering things and need my help or there are things that you do remember, I'm always here to talk.

MYRTLE *considers this. Pause.*

MYRTLE. Lemme ask you this, Rudy. If you was looking through a crack in a door and you could see ten people, would you think there are ten people on the other side or would you think there are a hundred?

RUDY. If I could only see ten through the crack, I'd think there were more than ten, yes.

MYRTLE. That's right. When you look back at our past, you're only ever seeing ten. There's a hundred more things that are forgotten. If you keep looking back to see what's behind you, you miss what's right here. You understand?

RUDY *processes this. Beat.* MELROSE *appears at the gate.*

RUDY. Nan? Are you gonna be okay with Jackie? You can call for her if –

MYRTLE. I don't need that woman.

RUDY. Just know you're not on your own, okay?

MYRTLE. I'm not. Your grandfather is here.

MYRTLE *nods to the gate.* RUDY *looks at* MELROSE.

RUDY. Oh. So he is. Hi... Granddad.

MELROSE *nods to him.* RUDY *gets up and kisses* MYRTLE *on the head. He then goes to the gate.*

MYRTLE. And where are you going?

RUDY. To Trinidad.

They smile at each other. He passes MELROSE *as he goes.*

MELROSE. And him is mad like him father too.

MYRTLE *laughs. The rustling in the tree can be heard again.*

MYRTLE. Where you been, Melrose?

MELROSE *goes to her, producing a bouquet of daffodils. She smiles, admiring them. He sits at the table with her.*

MELROSE. I've not been far, Myrtle.

MYRTLE. Well you is here now, that's what matters.

MELROSE. I… I can't stay.

MYRTLE. Of course you can stay.

MELROSE. No. I have to go. For good this time.

MYRTLE. What kinda foolishness? Why yuh come back in my house if you was only going to leave again? You get on my nerves, Melrose!

MELROSE. You get on my nerves, woman!

MYRTLE. Out order. You think me is just sitting here waiting for you to turn up? No sir!

MELROSE You always want a fight.

MYRTLE. Me? I don't like to fight.

MELROSE *laughs.*

It's true! I am not a fighter. I am soft.

MELROSE. You could start a fight in a room by yourself.

MYRTLE *laughs in spite of herself and then the two laugh together.* MELROSE *reaches into his jacket pocket and takes something out.*

I need you to keep something for me.

He hands it to her.

MYRTLE. Your wedding ring?

MELROSE. That night I left... You know, when I was sitting in this chair –

MYRTLE. I remember.

MELROSE. I wasn't able to say goodbye, Myrtle. I'm sorry. I owed you that. No one should have to be left without a goodbye.

MYRTLE. That's why you're here now?

MELROSE *nods.*

What must I do with this ring? It's yours.

MELROSE. You can bring it to me. All right?

MYRTLE. All right.

He takes her hand.

MELROSE. I love you.

MYRTLE *smiles at him.* MELROSE *gets up, goes to the garden gate and exits. Beat.*

EDDIE (*offstage*).
I've been a wild rover for many's the year
And I've spent all me money on whiskey and beer
But now I'm returning with gold in great store
And I never will play the wild rover no more

MYRTLE (*singing softly*).
And it's no, nay, never
No, nay never no more
Will I play the wild rover
No never no more.

MYRTLE *sits in silence for a moment before coming alive again, remembering something.*

But this wotless nurse! Jackie! Where you is? Jackie?

Beat.

I'm going out to come back.

MYRTLE *doesn't move. Slowly, she begins to doze off. After a while, the rustling is heard again.*

She opens her eyes before getting up and staring up into the tree.

Sarah? Ah you dat?

Her face lights up.

End of play.

A Nick Hern Book

Miss Myrtle's Garden first published in Great Britain in 2025 as a paperback original by Nick Hern Books Limited, The Glasshouse, 49a Goldhawk Road, London W12 8QP, in association with the Bush Theatre, London

Miss Myrtle's Garden copyright © 2025 Danny James King

Cover illustration by Isabella Cotier

Designed and typeset by Nick Hern Books, London
Printed in Great Britain by Mimeo Ltd, Huntingdon, Cambridgeshire PE29 6XX

A CIP catalogue record for this book is available from the British Library

ISBN 978 1 83904 477 9

www.nickhernbooks.co.uk/environmental-policy

Nick Hern Books' authorised representative in the EU is
Easy Access System Europe – Mustamäe tee 50, 10621 Tallinn, Estonia
email gpsr.requests@easproject.com

www.nickhernbooks.co.uk